CLOUD OF WITNESSES

Sisters of St. Joseph

of Rochester

REMEMBERED

WILLIAM H. SHANNON

CLOUD OF WITNESSES

Sisters of St Joseph

of Rochester

REMEMBERED

©2006 by William H. Shannon

ISBN 1-59872-698-6

To the Sisters of St. Joseph of Rochester

CONTENTS

SISTERS WHO SERVED IN LEADERSHIP ROLES

THE SISTERS OF NAZARETH COLLEGE

SISTERS IN VARIOUS MINISTRIES

INTRODUCTION

I have been associated with the Sisters of St. Joseph of Rochester for sixty years, and for the last twenty-five as Motherhouse chaplain. During this latter period I have been privileged to preach the funeral homily for many sisters who have gone to God. I can only hope that they will be rooting for me when the time comes for me to join them.

A number of people have suggested that these homilies be published. This book is at least a partial response to that request. Of the many homilies, I have selected fifty-five for publication in this book.

As the book goes to press, I want to express my gratitude to the Sisters of St. Joseph of Rochester for the joy and happiness that working with them has brought into my life.

I want also to thank Sister Mary Anne Turner for the invaluable help she has given in bringing this book to publication. The insertion of the photos of the sisters that accompany each homily took many hours of her time. She also designed the brilliant cover that adds special grace to this book. I wish also to express my thanks to Kathy Urbanic for locating the photos and for the careful proofreading of the text that she did so generously and so capably.

William H. Shannon

SISTERS WHO SERVED IN LEADERSHIP ROLES

MOTHER AGNES CECILIA TROY 10-5-2003

Readings: Rev. 19:5-9
1 Peter 1:18-25
Jn .10: 14-18

      Every time I visited Mother Agnes Cecilia during her final illness, I invited her to say the prayer we had both said so many times at her sister Jeanne's bedside as Jeanne was dying: "Come, Lord Jesus, come, Into your hands, O Lord, I commend my spirit." I well remember Jeanne's deathbed nine years ago. Toward the very end Jeanne said to me: "There is one thing I want you to do for me." "What is it, Jeanne?" I asked her. She said: "I want you to take care of my sister." As I look back over the years since Jeanne's death in Advent 1994, I can only hope that I have not failed the promise I made to Jeanne.

I do know that over the years Agnes Cecilia and I have had many wonderful conversations. At the time when this building was little more than a dream, we promised one another that, no matter what, we would make it here – and we both did. I also suggested that whoever of us died first, the other one would have to give the homily. I'm not sure she completely agreed with her part of the bargain, but I am happy that I can carry out my part. There is one conversation I shall never forget. I was alone with her for close to a half hour when she was at the Friendly Home. She told me about her spirituality. She quoted John of the Cross, Elizabeth of the Trinity as if they were true intimate friends. Never before had I realized the depths of her spirituality.

I must add one more personal note. Up till the time of the accident that put her into sick bed and eventually into the dying process, she had always called me "Father." All during this last illness, whenever she spoke to me, she addressed me simply as "Bill." Dying has a way of sweeping aside all that is non-essential.

We are here this afternoon to celebrate the story of Mother Agnes Cecilia. Everyone here, I suspect, has a part in that story as well as a story of your own to tell about your contact with her. By any standards, her story is a remarkable, truly amazing story. She was a woman born to command. This was amply illustrated, not only in her lifetime, but during her final days of her earthly existence. From her sick-bed she issued orders and they were obeyed. People knew the voice of authority when they heard it.

Because she was born to command, it was inevitable that the time would come when she would be elected to the highest office in the Congregation of the Sisters of St. Joseph.

Several weeks ago, the Congregation of the Sisters of St. Joseph gathered for a refounding meeting. Refounding of a congregation is not something that happens only once. I would want to suggest that the Congregation was refounded in 1963 when Agnes Cecilia became Mother Superior. Those who preceded her in that office – remarkable women though they were – belonged to a pre-modern tradition of religious life. It was a tradition in which, for all practical purposes, obedience had replaced love as the greatest of the virtues. It was a particular kind of obedience, too – not the rich understanding of obedience found in the scriptures, but an understanding that grew out of the limitations of seventeenth century French spirituality. The watchword of this way of viewing obedience was expressed in this type of expression: "Keep the rule and the rule will keep you. Be obedient to the will of your superior and you will be sure that you are doing the will of God."

Agnes Cecilia did not understand this kind of approach. She was a reasonable woman and also a loving person. I have been told that her first letter to the congregation was signed "Lovingly." With all due respect to her predecessors, it is difficult to think that any of them would have thought of ending a letter to the sisters in that fashion.

Agnes Cecilia was not a feminist, but she had an instinctive intuition of the feminine side of God. Her title may have been "Mother Superior," but in dealing with the sisters, it was always "Mother" not "Superior" that predominated. Her God was not the God of the Old Testament prophets, but the God Jesus revealed to us. The

God of Jesus who loves God's people passionately with a deep concern and heartfelt compassion for all.

If Pope John XXIII opened the widows of the Church, Agnes Cecilia brightened up the walls of the Motherhouse – a signal that she was going to brighten up the lives of the Sisters of St. Joseph. She treated sisters as individuals whose rights and dignity she respected. To her they were never "subjects." They were co-workers with her in the spread of God's kingdom.

Did you notice how unusual the readings are which Mother chose for this Mass? They are not the ordinary readings we generally hear at a funeral liturgy. I spent a lot of time just sitting with them, trying to figure out why she chose them. I came up with this possible answer. My thought is this. The first reading is about her hope for eternal joy – expressed in the symbol of being present at the wedding feast of the Lamb: the union of the risen Jesus with his own. And of course a reunion with her beloved Sister Jeanne, the thought of whom was never very far from her mind.

The second reading I see as her charge to the Congregation. This charge is summed up in that marvelous sentence: "Having purified our souls by our obedience to the truth, let us love one another deeply from the heart." Note the emphasis: obedience not first to her or to any superior, but obedience to the truth -- the truth that ultimately is God. Note, secondly, the repositioning of love at the center: "Let us love one another deeply from the heart." That is her parting gift to the Congregation which summed up her charge to them and her hope for the future when she would no longer be physically present with them.

Finally, why the Gospel of the Good Shepherd? Because it expressed what she wanted her style of leadership to be. The shepherd who cares for the sheep and loves each one of them as unique individuals and who especially cares for those who seem to stray – this set the model of her leadership and her on-going relationship with the Congregation. It is also a promise of her love and care for the Congregation that she will carry into eternity and will continue to exercise from heaven.

Elizabeth Johnson has written: "Love is the voice of eternity in our hearts." We must listen intently for that voice of eternity. Who knows? The voice we hear may well be the voice of Agnes Cecilia. May she rest in God's peace!

SR. ROSALMA HAYES 8-21-2003

Readings: Is. 61: 1-3, 10,11
Eph. 3: 14-21
Jn. 14: 1-8

We come here this evening to rejoice with Sr. Rosalma that she has achieved the ultimate goal of human life: entrance into the loving embrace of the God she served so faithfully and in so many marvelous and diverse ways. She has been welcomed into the heavenly dwelling place that Jesus has prepared for her. If we really understood what this means, this going home to God, we would be jumping up and down and shouting hosanna, hosanna or, maybe, hurrah, hurrah, hurray. Or perhaps: brava Rosalma! bravo Jesus! We can only try to imagine this experience of homecoming to the only true home that any of us can have. But even imagination cannot do it. As Paul puts it: 'Eye has not seen, ear has not heard, nor has the human mind been able to imagine what God has prepared for those who love him."

What he is telling us is that we all have wonderful experiences of things and places we see for the first time. Yesterday some of us went to the new St. Bernard's School of Ministry and Theology. Seeing the building from the road, I could not possibly have imagined the beauty and spaciousness and lightsomeness of this wonderful new center of learning. But that experience of wonder and surprise is as nothing compared to the experience that will be ours when Jesus comes to us and takes us to the place he has prepared for us.

So it is that we gather here tonight to rejoice with Sr. Rosalma that her life, new life, her real life, has just begun. But this funeral liturgy is more for us than for her. We come to celebrate, first the life eternal that she now lives, but also the mortal life that she lived among us. We are here tonight to reflect on that life-with-us and ask ourselves what we can learn from her and the many ministries to which she gave herself so completely. What would she want us to learn from her life among us? There will be, I am sure, a number of different answers.

Two things I suggest (among many others) we can learn from her. First, she calls us to become, like herself, total Americans. Sr. Rosalma belonged not to the Northern hemisphere alone or the Southern, but to both. She little realized this when, at the prophetical call of Mother Agnes Cecilia, she became the leader of the group of sisters who would go to Brazil in 1964. At their sending ceremony, they heard the words of Isaiah: The Spirit of the Lord has sent you to bring the good news to the oppressed, to bind up the broken-hearted, to proclaim liberty to those held captive." She and the sisters with her embarked on a journey into the unknown. What they discovered was a culture far different from our own and often embracing values our world had lost sight of. They discovered a church that they could easily link with the early primitive church: a church where people were poor and needy, but with hearts and minds open to the Gospel of love and mutual concern for one another. It was a church, oppressed and downtrodden for centuries, that was beginning to awaken. It was beginning to hear and eager to welcome the Gospel of liberation and freedom. It was a volcano waiting to erupt.

Whatever their initial motives, Sr. Rosalma and those who accompanied her (and those who came subsequently) would, I feel sure, agree with these words of Thomas Merton, written to Sr. Emmanuel, a Benedictine sister in Brazil: "The United States has no real appreciation of its relationship with Latin America and its obligation to Latin America. Still less of how much it needs Latin America culturally and spiritually." Yes, Rosalma's message to us, first of all, would be that we cannot be truly American until we become totally American; and, indeed, at a deeper level, her message to us is that we cannot be truly and totally Catholic unless we are open to what God is doing in cultures other than our own.

The second message that I think this woman of many journeys would want to give us is the realization her external journey, frequent as it was, was, at a deeper level, a symbol of the real journey of her life —which was internal: the ever growing journey toward the God who dwells in her heart. She could easily make her own the words Thomas Merton wrote to his friends, as he was about to embark on what would be his last journey: "Our real journey in life is interior: it is a matter of growth, deepening and an ever greater surrender to the creative action of love and grace in our hearts."

This is clearly the reason she chose as one of the readings for this Mass a section from St. Paul's Epistle to the Ephesians. Nowhere in the Bible could you find a better description of what the interior life means. With Paul, she prays for us (and I paraphrase) she prays: that we may be strengthened in our inner deepest self by the power of God's Spirit. She prays: that Christ may dwell in our hearts through faith. She prays: that our lives may be rooted and grounded in love. She prays: that we may experience powerfully the breadth and length and height and depth of the love Christ has for us. She prays: that we may be filled with all the fullness of God. What a program of interiority! What a goal to strive for! That 4th chapter of Ephesians is the final gift she would offer us.

As some of you know, when in 1982 I went to Brazil, I learned to speak Portuguese quite fluently. So on this occasion I would be amiss if I didn't say something in Portuguese -- for those of us who understand it. I have to admit, though, that my fluency in the language extends to a quite limited vocabulary. To be specific, my vocabulary consists of one word "obrigado," which means "thank you" and one phrase which I learned because I had arrived on New Year's Eve. The phrase was: "feliz ano novo." "Happy New Year!" For this funeral I added two more word to my vocabulary. So I shall conclude by saying to Irma Rosalma: Obrigado! Obrigado! Feliz vida nova! Feliz vida nova!

Sr. Dorothy Agnes Tyrrell   1-8-2002

Readings: 1 Cor. 13: 8-13
Jn. 14: 1-6

This has been, I think, the hardest homily that I have ever prepared. Not that there wasn't much to say. But how to find words to say it? In other words, how to give a homily about a saint? I had to ask myself: What would Sr. Dorothy Agnes want me to say this afternoon, as we celebrate her life and ministry? She herself chose the readings for this liturgy. So I had to ask myself: what does she want us to hear and learn from these readings? I think that maybe she might tell me to say something like this:

"Tell everybody it's true. Yes, Jesus has indeed prepared a place here for me -- with God. I'd like to tell you about it, but human language just isn't capable of handling it. Just know that the experience surpasses all you have ever hoped for or dreamed about. But also I really want you to realize that I haven't left you. I say this because I am not really in some other place: I am in God. But so are you. Thus, we are still together – in God. You don't realize that as fully as I do now. But it is so wonderfully true. And some day you will have that full realization too.

"Tell them [I think she would have said to me] to love one another. Tell them that that is all that really matters. Faith and hope will yield to knowledge and fulfillment, but love will always remain. That is really what heaven means – being in God and since God is love, being in God means always being in Love. You are already there, but you don't realize it fully, because you only see a mirror reflection of it. But someday you're going to experience Reality Itself. You will experience God in the most wonderful way, as I already do.

"Tell them to pray for me, if it makes them feel better. But frankly, I would prefer to have them pray with me. "Tell them too that I'm going to see about hastening that new motherhouse to completion. I'm not sure I was much help to the College in building that last dormitory, but now I'm in a position of greater influence."

A good part of Sr. Dorothy Agnes ministry, as I am sure you know, was spent at Nazareth College. I spoke to a faculty member yesterday and asked: "What do you remember about Sr. Dorothy Agnes? Without a moment's hesitation she said: "I remember the twinkle in her eye." I couldn't help but think how appropriate that comment was. When you spoke with her there was a sparkle in her eyes: a sparkle that I can only think was an outward expression of a beauty shining out from the inside. Quite simply put, she loved God. And it showed. People knew it. That is what this college faculty member meant when she went on further to say: "When you were with Sister Dorothy Agnes, you felt you were in the presence of God." And of course you were. There was a transparency about her that enabled you to see God when you saw her. The beauty of God shone through in her actions and in who she simply was as a person and as a Sister of St. Joseph.

During the last couple of weeks we have been reading at Mass from the first letter of John – a work produced in a community in the early Church that was unique. It was an egalitarian community, led by the Spirit, where the bond that joined them together was the love they had for one another. There was one person in that community who is never named, but who was seen as the one who embodied the life of that community at its very best. That person is called "the beloved disciple." Sandra Schneiders in her wonderful book on the Gospel of John offers the interesting possibility that the "beloved disciple" may have been Mary Magdalene. I'll leave you to yourselves to find out why she thinks this. I simply mention it because I have the conviction that, if we wanted to designate someone in the Congregation who in her own life embodied the life of the Congregation at its best, we would not go far wrong in thinking of Sr. Dorothy Agnes as "the beloved disciple" of the Congregation of the Sisters of St. Joseph.

In attempting to describe her as "the beloved disciple" of the Congregation, I looked to the "Maxims of the Little Design." I was amazed that there were a hundred of them and that you all knew them by heart – at one time. I don't think I ever read them before, but I must say that there really is a good bit of solid spirituality in them, though they might need a bit of contemporary tweaking. As I read them, I saw several that I felt captured the spirit of Sr. Dorothy Agnes. I finally decided on one that I think embodied her spirituality in the clearest possible way. It was Maxim 52 which says: "Interpret all things from the best possible point of view." I can remember some of you who were in the juniorate under her telling how, if you had broken a rule and had to go to her for a penance, you never had to make excuses for yourself. She did that for you. She would say to you: "Now, dear, you really didn't intend to do this, did you?" And you were quite ready to agree with her.

But this maxim means much more than escape from a penance. "Interpreting all things from the best possible point of view" is sign of a wisdom that can see below the surface into the deepest reality of another person – that sees beyond the disguises that people put on and the illusions they live by -- their inner reality, their true self, the self that is untouched by sin or evil, the self that is one with God and known fully only to God. If only we could see that reality in one another, we would be filled with so much awe that we would want to fall down and worship one another.

"To interpret all things in the best possible way" – what richness that would bring to community. What changes it would bring even to casual conversations. I won't even attempt to say how different politics and business would be if politicians and businessmen interpreted all things in the best possible way. What if Republicans put the best possible interpretation on what Democrats did and vice versa. It is probably asking too much of them. But is it too much to ask of people who claim to be disciples of Jesus Christ, who truly believe that he is "the way and the truth and the life?"

Of course to put this principle into practice makes big demands on us. It calls for the marvelous simplicity of life – something that Sr. Dorothy Agnes had so beautifully. Simplicity is overcoming the divisions in ourselves so that we become single-minded enough that we can live a unified life. This is what the desert fathers and mothers called purity of heart. Purity of heart means above all being willing to let go of all that divides us, of all that is illusory, all that is false in us.

Sr. Dorothy Agnes was one of the freest persons I have ever known. She knew that true freedom comes not with hanging on, but with being willing to let go. And the final letting go is the letting go of this mortal life into the embrace of a loving God. And Dorothy Agnes was eager for that final letting go. One of papers that Sr. Margaret Charles found in the prayer book Sr. Dorothy Agnes bequeathed to her was a prayer she had copied from Teilhard de Chardin's book *The Divine Milieu*:

When the signs of age begin to mark my body and still more when they touch my mind); when the ill that is to diminish me or carry me off strikes from without or is born within me; when the painful moment comes in which I suddenly awaken to the fact that I am ill or growing old; and above all at that last moment when I feel I am losing hold of myself and am absolutely passive within the hands of the great unknown forces that have formed me -- in all those dark moments, O God, grant that I may understand that it is You (provided only my faith is strong enough) who are painfully parting the fibers of my being in order to penetrate to the very marrow of my substance and bear me away within Yourself.

Under this quotation, in her own tiny but elegant handwriting, she wrote her own addition to this wonderful prayer. Here is what she wrote: "Teach me to treat my death as an act of communion."

SR. HILDA MURPHY 5-26-1995

Readings: 1 Corinthians 2: 1-10
John 21: 15:19

     I entered under Sr. Thomasina; so I was never under Sr. Hilda's direction as a postulant. Actually, as I recall it, I was living on the novitiate side of the house when Sr. Hilda became mistress of postulants. In fact I lived there for about nine years. But nobody ever asked me to take vows or receive the habit.

     I did get the discipline every week, though. Every Saturday afternoon, just as I was prepared to take a nap, those infernal polishing machines that were used on the linoleum floor kept banging against the door and the wall of my room. You can understand why there was a deep psychological need in me to have the motherhouse floors carpeted.

And of course, whenever there was a congregational retreat, Mother Rose Miriam graciously gave me a vacation. I don't mean a paid vacation. She just told me to get out of my room so that the retreat master would have a place to stay. I have always been grateful to Mother Rose for this, because it helped to build up in me the humility of which I am so rightly proud.

Sr. Hilda was a very gracious lady, a woman of deep prayer and learning. (I learned just the other day that she had a degree in both Latin and Greek. That's pretty classy, you have to admit.) Sr. Hilda deeply loved the young girls who were put in her charge. I really believe that those who had her as postulants know that (or at least I hope they do). Some might say: if she loved us, she used strange ways to show that love.

But, let's be honest, it was not a good time in the Church to be in a position of authority, especially a lesser position. It was almost as if they had to give up their own personality and their personal warmth and take on a role. And it was a role for which they had no training. Being appointed took the place of training

They had a deep sense of the seriousness of their responsibility to mould their subjects into something like Agnes the fervent novice. (I'm still trying to find that book and I am beginning to wonder whether it ever really existed.) They felt it their duty to discipline their "subjects," to break wills that could be obstinate and self-seeking. At all costs they had to root out pride and make these young people humble.

What they did not realize – and there was no one to teach it to them – was that this mentality smacked of Pelagianism: this feeling that they had to make their subjects virtuous. They had to make them saints.

What this means is that in the atmosphere in which they operated at that time, they felt obligated to take upon themselves the task of doing what only the Holy Spirit and the grace of God can do. They did not do this out of pride but because they felt it was their responsibility and that they were accountable before God to accomplish this.

It may have been hard for those who were their subjects. What we perhaps don't realize, it may have been even harder for them.

The funny thing about it was that, even though we may see it now as the wrong way, somehow it worked: wonderful people came out of the system. It worked, not because the system was right, but because the grace of God can somehow make things come out right no matter what the system. Many wonderful, loving, self-sacrificing sisters came out of the postulancy directed by Sr. Hilda. And, in the mysterious operating of God's grace, it was through Sr. Hilda that this happened.

I really did not come to know Sr. Hilda till I became chaplain at the Motherhouse in 1980 and I always experienced her as a gracious, loving, kindly, well-read and, yes, liberal minded person. And it was so sad to see her in her last days when she was no longer herself. Externally, that is. What she was interiorly in those last years we cannot know. There are areas of the spiritual unconscious about which we simply have no knowledge or at best very little knowledge.

The fact that a person may have lost contact with what we blithely call the "real world," may actually mean that she is in touch with an inner world far more important and far more truly real than the world we label as "real."

During this time of preparation for Pentecost, the liturgy calls us to reflect on the Spirit of God who, according to the 4th Gospel, abides in us. Thus in John 14: 17, Jesus says of the Holy Spirit: "You know him because the Spirit abides with you and is in you." Later in the same chapter: "The Spirit will teach you everything and will remind you of all that I have said to you." (14:26)

What so often distracts us from hearing God's Spirit within us is the feverish activity that so often fills our lives. Merton has a poem that speaks of that interiority in which , as he puts it, we experience the "voice of a new world," "where Christ and angels walk among us everywhere."

Seized in the talons of the terrible Dove,
The huge unwounding Spirit,
We suddenly escape the drag of earth
Fly from the dizzy paw of gravity
And swimming in the wind that lies beyond the track
Of thought and genius and of desire,
Trample the white, appalling stratosphere

May we not say that it was in this spiritual stratosphere of deep interiority that Sr. Hilda dwelt in those last seemingly dark days? Did she there come to realize that God had accepted the gift of the many phases of her life? Did she there find the joy of the Risen Jesus and the peace that only he can give? It makes so much sense to think that she did. For, while she may have been for a time the prisoner of a way of understanding religious life that has now passed away and all of us were in that same prison), what really matters is that even the confines of a narrow understanding of religious life did not prevent her from the wholehearted giving of her life to God. And that is really what faith and religious life are all about.

THE SISTERS OF NAZARETH COLLEGE

SR. AGNES PATRICIA BREEN 7-7-1979
(LAST OF THE FOUNDING SISTERS)

A Valiant Woman has died. Sr. Agnes Patricia has gone home to God. She has entered into the place of joy and happiness that Jesus promised to prepare for her. We rejoice that she is making a new beginning of life in the presence of the Lord. All through life she sought his presence; now for the first time she experiences it, with all the veils and darkness removed.

And if I may be for the moment overly anthropomorphic about heaven, I can imagine what happened when she arrived there. I can see Sr. Raphael waiting with St. Peter and saying to her: It's about time you came. I have missed you. No one here knows how to take care of me as you did. I thought you'd never take that final step.

And I am sure that behind Sr. Raphael were Sr. Teresa Marie, and Sr. Rose Miriam and Sr. Rose Marie. And now that the five of them are together again, they are probably organizing the Nazareth College of the Beyond. After all, even some of the saints had a few rough edges that need to be smoothed off and refined. And I can't think of five people better able to do this than those five intrepid women who rejoice now that they have been reunited in the presence of the Lord. And Sr. Agnes Patricia may well have her goat, Club, as she had in the early days of the College (For the uninitiated the Goat, Club was a group of incorrigibles who were always getting into difficulties from which Aggie Pat had to extricate them.)

Actually, of course, we have no experience of heaven. If we try to talk about it at all, it has to be in terms of our experiences here on earth. We have no understanding of what it really means to pass over into the happiness that God has in store for those who have served Him in faithfulness and love.

Yet we believe in the Communion of Saints. We believe, therefore, that those who go before us are reunited in the Holy One with those whom they knew and loved on earth. We believe, moreover, that they carry with them into God's presence the concerns and loves that motivated them while they were still among us. That is why I know and you know that Sr. Agnes Patricia is still very proud of, very much interested in and very much concerned about the College that she helped to found.

We recall her memory today not so much for her sake as for ours. Going back 55 years ago to the beginnings of Nazareth College puts us in touch with a special source of strength and power.

There is always a special power connected with beginnings. The beginning is the moment of creative power: the special power that comes from bringing into existence something that never was before. Beginnings carry with them the special power of seeing goals and directions with a lucidity of vision and a singleness of purpose that sometimes can get lost as time goes on.

It is because of this power of beginnings that the Jews in their worship continually return to the Exodus Event, the story of their beginnings. They celebrate Passover, so that the strength of their beginnings may be poured into them to renew them.

That is why we Christians celebrate the Eucharist as the memorial of the Lord's death and resurrection. For this event marked our beginning as a Christian people, and we celebrate it in the Eucharist so that we may always be in touch with our origins and be renewed and strengthened by this regular contact with our beginnings.

The deepest meaning of the Second Vatican Council in the Church is not simply that it has produced changes in the Church that were very much needed. The real achievement of the Council and the Post-Councilor period is that it has returned us to the Gospel. It has returned us to our beginnings, not in any antiquarian way, but in a way that has enabled us to experience the strength and insights that come to us from our beginnings.

Just as the synagogue and the Church have to return periodically to the time of beginnings, so does an institution, like a college.

A College must continually celebrate its beginnings. It must continually measure itself against the goals and purposes of those who brought it into being. This is not to say that a College should not grow and expand its goals; yet it does mean that it must always renew itself at the source out of which it sprang. For there is a special power in beginnings.

The five women who founded Nazareth College were well-educated women who wanted to share a culture of faith that meant so much to them. They wanted to create a community of learning - made up of younger and older scholars, dedicated to truth in all its aspects and dedicated to wisdom that refuses to let truth get fragmented. They were interested in refinement and sensitivity to all that was good and noble in the human spirit. They had no computers. Students were not numbers, they were persons individually known, respected, guided and loved.

We now have computers at Nazareth College and every student has a number. I'm not suggesting that this is bad, but simply that it is all the more reason for us to return to our beginnings and renew our dedication to the insights of our founders: to renew our dedication to a personalism that loves and respects each student and faculty member and that builds a true community of learning concerned with the pursuit of truth and wisdom. Today we rejuvenate ourselves at our source.

When the last of the apostles died in the Church, there must have been a very special sense of loss. The last link connecting the Christian community with the immediate experience of the Christ-Event was gone. From that moment on the Church had to live on the memories of her beginnings as they are inscribed in the Scriptures and in her living tradition.

It is something of this kind of loss that we experience today, as the last of the founders of Nazareth College is taken from our midst. This sense of loss must be accompanied by a determination not to forget, a determination to continue forging a living tradition that will always link us with the experience of our beginnings - those moments of great power and strength and insight.

I haven't said very much about Sr. Agnes Patricia. I think she would not want me to. She never wanted a fuss made over her. She was a gentle woman, who was a quiet tower of strength. She was a woman of great faith and fidelity. When the occasion arose in the life of the College that her faith was put to the test, she weathered that test with equanimity and without bitterness. She was a selfless person, too much concerned with others to spend much time thinking about herself.

She was Valiant Woman who, because she followed the Way has entered into the fullness of Truth and the Life. We can only rejoice as she makes a new beginning with Him who is the Alpha and Omega, the Beginning and the End. We can only rejoice that she has been given the reward of her labors. "Let her works praise her at the city gates."

NAZARETH COLLEGE – THE GREAT STORY
delivered at Nazareth College 5-1-1991

We come together this afternoon to reflect on the Nazareth Story and to pay honor and respect to three sisters: Sister Rose Angela, Sister Margaret Teresa, and Sister Teresa Ann, who during the combined century plus of their years at Nazareth, contributed their particular stories to the Nazareth Story. For theirs is the Great Story of Nazareth College, which is the ongoing, unbroken story of this collegial community, as it has moved from its foundations in 1924 to the present reality it is.

In this Great Story are contained the particular stories of Nazareth, as over the years students, faculty, administration and staff have incorporated their own stories into the living stream of the Great Story.

We are here today to remember three wonderful sisters. Because there is a special power in beginnings and because, though not founders of the College, they were close to them in time, their particular stories contributed significantly to the Great Story. Their Nazareth – say, the Nazareth of the '40's, '50's and '60's – differed in many ways from the Nazareth that all of you know now - you whose stories are even now being written into the pages of the Great Story. I hope you will indulge me a bit of nostalgia, as I recall some of the lighter moments of the Nazareth of their day (and mine, too).

Today is the first of May and May in those days meant May Day. It meant the crowning of the Queen of the May and the dance about the Maypole, set up on the ground to the north of Smyth Hall. May also meant graduation and all students were expected (that meant "required") to stay for graduation; and each class entertained the graduates on different days. The events of graduation began on a Saturday and concluded the following Wednesday, which was the day the degrees were awarded. The fall of the year saw the old gymnasuim (now the cabaret) transformed for one night into a Viennese ballroom, with mirrors on the walls, blue lights on the tables, and young women in their flowing gowns waltzing (generally not very well) with their dates into the night. And of course there was a special place at the dance for the sisters where they could greet the young women and their dates. Yes, dates. That was a problem during the war, World War II, that is. So for school dances we imported men from the Naval base at Sampson, and they came in bus loads.

Those were the days when all the resident students fit into Medaille dining room. They were expected (again read "required") to dress for dinner, which was always served to them. Then there was the Christmas dinner for all the students, after which the Glee Club sang the Messiah. And Bishop Kearney would be there; and it was always his delight to add an extra day (or two, or more) to the Christmas holidays. There were the St. Patrick's Day skits, each year getting more and more elaborate, and the weekly student hours, always on Thursday afternoon, that everyone was expected to attend. And there was the St. Thomas Aquinas symposium each year on his feast day, in which the philosophy majors spoke learnedly and eloquently about the *philosophia perennis*. And nobody paid any attention to me when I stoutly tried to assert that St. Thomas was a theologian, not a philosopher.

Each week on Wednesday, every resident student was expected (read "required") to attend Mass at the Motherhouse Chapel at 7:00 a.m., wearing academic gowns and caps. And everyone wondered what mysterious realities those academic gowns must have covered at so early an hour in the morning. And, oh yes, there were the curfews: 7:30 p.m. on weekdays each resident student had to be in her room. On weekends the curfew was a "generous" 11:00 p.m., but that applied not to the whole weekend, but to two of the three days only. Many students maintained that through their four years at Nazareth, they never saw the ending of a movie, because just as the climactic moment of the movie came, they had to leave to catch the 10:30 bus to get back to campus by 11:00. Those were the days when maybe a dozen envied students drove to school in their own automobiles. The rest took the bus.

And I could go on with the light side of the story of those yesteryears, when Sister Rose Angela was Dean, when Sister Margaret Teresa managed to get every freshman (or almost everyone) to love Dante and loved him so much herself that she began to look like the statue of him that graced her always colorful classroom. And Sister Teresa Anne, with her warm smile, greeted graciously all who came to visit Nazareth. She was a one-person hospitality committee.

The Nazareth whose lighter side I have tried to describe may seem light-years removed from the Nazareth of today. Yet, while so many things are different, there is a continuity. It is to be found in the Great Story that takes into itself the particular stories of various years. For the Great Story is the Tradition of Nazareth College. Rooted in the vision and wisdom of the past, it is yet living and ever young, with something peculiarly new and original to say to people of today. That Tradition, which is the Big Story, is something which is always old and yet at the same time ever new, because it is always being revivified. It is born again in each generation of Nazareth folk, to be lived and applied in new and particular ways. This Big Story, this Tradition, teaches us how to live, because it develops and expands our powers of mind, heart and faith. It also shows us how to give ourselves as a leaven and a challenge to the world in which we live.

One of the most heartening things I have heard about Nazareth in very recent days is the support and love and concern that the whole Nazareth community has extended to one of their number who, following his conscience, opposed the war in the Persian Gulf and felt called to express his opposition through an act of civil disobedience; for which, I might add, he is being punished by the law far beyond what is in any way reasonable. Yes, my heart was warmed when I heard of the compassion and solidarity with him that the Nazareth community gave and is giving to Harry Murray. And as I thought of it, my mind went back, almost 30 years, to a particular point, a particular day in fact, in the ongoing Great Story of Nazareth. It was in the later years of the '60s'. It was the day the president of the Nazareth student government went to the president of the college and said: "We are calling off all classes tomorrow. We are going to have seminars and discussions about the war in Vietnam. We need to be alive to moral and political issues that are involved in that war. We need to act as a student body."

I couldn't help but think that, yes, the time and the settings and the issues are different, but the sense of community and the need for enlightenment, the sense of commitment and compassion – these were present in both these stories. They have been and are and, please God, will continue to be the dynamic elements of that continuity which will incorporate the particular stories of different moments into the unity of the One Great Story which is Nazareth.

SISTER ROSE ANGELA NOONAN 1-5-1991

Readings: Ephesians 1: 3-10
Matthew 11: 25-30

Sr. Rose Angela and I "came into office," if I may put it that way, at the same time. In the summer of 1949 she was appointed to succeed Sr. Teresa Marie as the Dean of Nazareth College. That same summer I was appointed chaplain to succeed Fr. Lintz, who, though he continued to teach, had taken charge of a mission church in Marion, New York.

A lot of adjectives spring to my mind when I think of Sr. Rose Angela: gracious, kindly, warm-hearted, affable, cordial, generous, thoughtful, wholesome. They are all adjectives that express a certain gentility, a kind of primordial innocence, a sense of refinement, a ladylike elegance. The Pittsford Fire Department could witness to her gentility. One night, fairly early in the evening, she was in her office. Someone called her and said that a fire had started in the trash can in that store room that was below the dressing room off the stage in the old gym. Sister called the Pittsford Fire Department: "This is Sr. Rose Angela from Nazareth College. It seems we have a little fire over here. We would be obliged if you would please come and take care of it for us. And please do come quietly. Some of the Sisters at the Motherhouse have already retired, and we wouldn't want to awaken them, would we?" They came, put out the fire and were as quiet as fallen snow.

Sr. Rose Angela had a great sense of humor. I remember one occasion when several students at Le Puy Dorm planned a prank. They put a ladder outside the window of an upstairs bathroom and locked the bathroom from the inside. The next morning there was great upset on campus at the possibility that a young man had entered the house during the night. The police were called in and there was much excitement. I had just heard of the incident when one of the students came into my office, ostensibly to tell me about it. Actually she looked as guilty as Eve with a half-eaten apple in her hand. Finally I said: "Did you mastermind this?" She gulped: "Yes," and told me that there had been no young man. It was just a prank. I said: "You will have to go and tell Sr. Rose Angela." "Oh, no," she said, "I'll be sent home." Finally she agreed to go. A few minutes later, she was back, quite bewildered. She said: "I told Sr. Rose Angela and when I finished, she leaned back in her chair and laughed and laughed and laughed."

And Sister was an idealist and I mean that in the sense that Plato was an idealist. For Plato there was a realm of immutable archetypes in another world that were the models to which all temporal reality must conform. Things were real insofar as they corresponded to their archetype.

Sr. Rose Angela had an archetypal idea of what every Nazareth woman should be. The theme of many of her class meetings and student hours was precisely that: the kind of young lady that a Nazareth College student is expected to be. And because she was not sure that she was getting the picture across as clearly as she would have liked, at one point she brought in a woman from some charm school to teach the students how to conduct themselves as ladies. Of course Fr. Lintz and I got the lessons second-hand from the students. They taught us how to walk, how to curtsy, and how to take off our hand gloves and all sorts of other things that I can't even remember--all this relayed from charm class. Nazareth became Camelot for a brief time.

Yet I would not want to give the wrong impression. Her idea of what a Nazareth woman should be was not simply a matter of external show. She knew that ethics was much more important than etiquette and grace more important than charm. Still, she had the deep realization that the externals of a life are an expression of what is inside. She firmly believed that Nazareth college women were special: that the grace of God was in them and it needed to be expressed in a graceful way.

All of which is to say that she believed deeply in the significance of the great mystery of the incarnation which we have been celebrating these days, as she has been patiently waiting to go to God. She believed that grace was a constant factor in the Christian life and something that was especially active in the lives of young people. She really believed what Paul says in the first reading of our liturgy.

On Thursday morning Sr. Mary Paul showed me the readings which Sr. Rose Angela had chosen for this Mass. Her choice for the first reading is that magnificent passage from Ephesians, and she had typed it, or had it typed, and it was moving to me to see how she had written in her own, easily recognizable, hand at the end of this reading from Ephesians: "This is the Word of the Lord."

She wanted all of us to know that this is what she believed and this is what she wanted to say to all the Nazareth College women and indeed to all of us: God chose you, before the world began, to be holy and without blemish. God chose you to be full of joy. God wanted you to be God's children, as Christ was God's Child. The richness of God's grace has been lavished upon us. For we have been redeemed by Christ and are destined for union with God.

Sr. Rose Angela's instructions to the homilist for her funeral Mass were to speak about "our gratitude for redemption." This was the Word of God for her. And it was the Word she wanted to communicate to the women of Nazareth. I suggested earlier that she had an ideal of what the Nazareth woman should be, almost like Plato had a kind of archetypal form for all phenomenal reality. But actually the ideal she proposed was not Platonic; it was a Gospel ideal. It was an ideal based on the good news announced in the Christmas Mass: "The grace of God has appeared offering salvation to all peoples."

Realizing this, we can see that her emphasis on external ladylike deportment and carriage was simply an example of *noblesse oblige*. What we do and how we act express the reality that we are persons redeemed by Christ. True charm in acting and relating to others is not a substitute for grace, but a beautiful outpouring of the inner reality of a grace-filled soul. This is what she asked of Nazareth women. Some may have thought she asked for too much. But it was part of her uniqueness that she was ever calling people to rise to her own stature. Now she stands tall among the saints of God, full of gratitude for the wondrous gift of redemption.

SR. TERESA ANN WENDELGASS 3-20-1991

Readings: Isaiah 59: 21- 60: 1
Romans 8: 5-11
Luke 10: 21-22

Every once in a while in life you come upon a person who is very special because she is so very ordinary. A person who doesn't need to put on airs, because she doesn't take herself that seriously. A person who down deep is so fully in possession of herself that she doesn't have to try to prove anything by her actions. She is quite content to be the person God made her and sees no need of trying to be someone else. She is simple, straight-forward. She never dissembles. Anyone who has met such a person has come upon a precious treasure indeed. And I want to say tonight that that is the kind of person we recognized in Sr. Teresa Ann. Simple, wonderfully ordinary, never putting on any airs. It was a glorious thing that she was waked on St. Joseph's Day. I can just hear her in her humility and simplicity, saying: "I don't want all this fuss being made over me on St. Joseph's Day."

When Sr. Mary Paul asked me for scripture readings for Sister Teresa Ann's Mass, many scripture texts flooded my mind. One of the first ones I thought of was the story in John's Gospel where Philip introduces his friend Nathaniel to Jesus. Jesus looks at Nathaniel and he knows immediately that here is somebody very special: someone straight-forward, honest, gentle, with never any deceit in his heart. Jesus looks on him and says: "Behold an Israelite in whom there is no guile." That is our usual translation. The Revised English Bible conveys much more clearly what Jesus meant to say. It puts it this way: "Here is an Israelite worthy of the name; there is nothing false in him."

In speaking of Sr. Teresa Ann, I want to paraphrase Jesus' words about Nathaniel and say: "Here is a Christian worthy of the name; here is a Sister of St. Joseph worthy of the name; there is nothing false in her."

I thought, too, of Paul's moving hymn about love in First Corinthians. The love he speaks of is one that is utterly forgetful of self. Paul piles up adjectives to describe this selfless love: it is patient; it never envies, never boasts, never is conceited, never quick to take offense, always delights in the truth. I couldn't help but think that that hymn about love could be a hymn about Teresa Ann.

Finally, I decided on the Gospel reading from Luke, in which Jesus shows that complete reversal of values which is proper to the kingdom. The deepest things of the spirit are often hidden from the learned and the clever-- because so often their attention is on themselves. Most often God reveals the deepest realities of the spirit to those who are simple and genuine, those who don't give much thought to themselves, because their mind and heart are intent on God.

Sr. Teresa Ann was asked by God to carry a big cross. So often she had seizures of coughing that she could not control. Her breath became labored and difficult. So often normal breathing was impossible for her.

There is a close link between breathing and living. Indeed, before medical science developed more sophisticated ways of determining death, the oldest way of knowing that a person was dead was to hold a mirror to that person's mouth. If the mirror was unblurred, the person was dead. Death meant that the person had taken his/her last breath.

That is a physiological way of looking at death: it is the cessation of breathing. But as people of faith, we have another way of viewing death. In faith we believe that death, which is a ceasing of breathing and therefore the end of earthly life, is, in a theological sense, a Passover to new life, in which there is a wholly different kind of breathing. Death is learning to breathe in a new way. It is the joyful unlabored breathing of the Spirit.

The Greek word used in the New Testament for the Holy Spirit is the Greek word *pneuma*. *Pneuma* is a rich word that has many meanings. At the created level it's primary meaning is breath" or "wind." It can also be used to designate one's inner disposition of character. Thus, we might speak of a person as being in "good spirits" or in "bad spirits."

But most often when the word *pneuma* is used in the New Testament, it is used to refer to God or to participation in God's Life, in God's "Breathing." Referred to God, it means the "Holy Spirit" or, if you will, the "Holy Breath."

Before last Saturday, the word *pneuma* meant for Sr. Teresa Ann the difficult, labored breath that she so often had to put up with. But now, the word *pneuma*, "spirit", takes on the highest possible meaning for her. It is God's Spirit, the Holy Spirit in whom she now dwells. She has been taken into God. It is God's Spirit, God's Breath as it were, that breathes in her now. Now, fully one with God, it is God's Breath that has become her own Breath.

Our second reading -from Romans-- contrasts life in this world, which is life in the flesh, and the new life that Teresa Ann now lives. We can apply to her, in the profoundest way, Paul's words: "You are in the Spirit, since the Spirit of God dwells in you." The Holy Breath of God dwells in you. We can also say: "Rejoice, Teresa Ann, for what God has hidden from the learned and the clever, he now reveals to you. Enter into this JOY of the Breath of the Spirit."

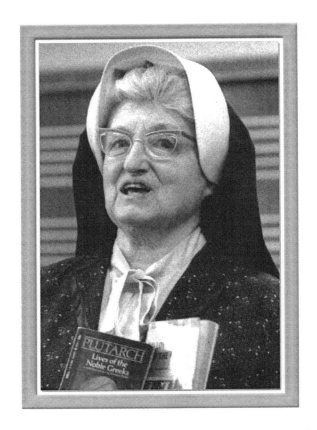

SR. MARGARET TERESA KELLEY 3-3-1991

Readings: Song of Songs 2: 10-13
Revelation 22: 12-14, 16-17, 20
John 1: 35-51

Sr. Margaret Teresa was an example of someone who was "in the world, but not of the world." And even the world she was in was not the world most people are in. So many people live in a world of illusion --staying always on life's surface, never reaching down into its depths, so often searching for goals that in the end turn out to be dust and ashes. Sr. Margaret Teresa was in touch with the real world, the world of truth and goodness. She lived in the depths of life --and often you had to call her out of those depths to do very ordinary things--such as going to eat dinner at night, when she may have gotten herself engrossed in some book and completely forgotten the time. That's why her conversation was at times abrupt. She would come out with some thought which seemed to have nothing to do with where you were at the time. But it was something she had been dwelling on. And when the idea that she had been mulling over came to fruition, she spoke it to whomever was fortunate enough to be there at the time, just assuming that that person must have been going through the same kind of thinking also.

One might almost say that she walked in the world of essences: she always searched for the roots of things, their hidden being, their true reality. Her books helped her. That is why, when she came to the St. Joseph's Convent Infirmary and was told she could not take all her books with her, she said: "Fine. I will just take the ones that are essential." And the box was duly marked "essential books," and I'm sure she could have given the reason why each of them was essential.

Those who took her classes had unforgettable experiences. There was a simplicity about her teaching methods. No one who had to dress up and play the role of a pilgrim on the way to Canterbury ever forgot about Chaucer and his tales. And everybody knows that it was said that the more she taught Dante, the more she began to look like that splendid statue of him in her classroom. And the funny thing is that it was true! And her classroom was a delight to visit. It was like going into a museum, a museum where certain things were fixed and permanent -- like the map of the arduous paths up Mount Carmel, for instance, but other things were regularly changed. Sr. Jamesetta told me how one of the watchmen at the college told her that every once in a while he would look into Margy's room to see what the new decorations were.

Two weeks ago I received a letter from Barbara Gurney from some town in Kansas. She was a Nazareth graduate of 1950 – an English major. She wrote to say that she had decided to go to graduate school – after the passage of 41 years! She needed a letter of recommendation from a former teacher. Would I write one? To prod my memory a bit, she recalled a few things about herself at Nazareth. One of the things she told me was about Sr. Margaret Teresa and myself. Barbara was something of a rebel, and in one of Sr. Margaret Teresa's classes, her assignment was to do an essay. She chose Martin Luther as her subject. When she handed in her paper, Sr. Margaret Teresa, not sure which realm of the Divine Comedy Martin Luther belonged in --remember we were not then in an ecumenical age--told Barbara to bring her essay to me, and I would correct it! So that was something I did for her, but mostly she was doing things for me.

And I can attest to the fact that she was a wonderful proofreader. She read articles and books for me, and discovered mistakes that no one else was able to detect. And sometimes I received a gentle lesson on a word's proper meaning or on the correct form of punctuation. The reason she was so good a proofreader and also why I liked to have her proofreading my writing was a love we shared --- a love for words. Words must not be used carelessly, because there is something sacred about them: they are windows to reality and they are tiny fragments of the One who is the Word of God. I shall miss her generous assistance and the wonderful conversations it occasioned.

One of the sisters at 4141 East Avenue told me about one of those abrupt, right-into-the middle-of-things conversations she had with Sister Margaret Teresa and it had to do with the wondrous reality of words. Sr. Margaret Teresa asked her: "What is the most beautiful word in the Bible?" And very quickly she answered her own question. [In parenthesis, I want to say that it would be interesting to put her question to everybody here and see what words we might come up with.] Her answer was spoken without hesitation. "The most beautiful word in the Bible," she said is: "COME."

Think of the many times this word occurs just in the Gospels. "COME to me all you who are weary and find life burdensome, and I will refresh you." (Mt 12:28) When the disciples-to-be question Jesus about where he is staying, his answer, which can be read at many levels, is "COME, and see." (John 1:39) When Peter sees Jesus walking on the water, Peter wants to join him: "Bid me come to you across the water." Jesus simply says to him: "COME."(Mt 14:28) Then there are Jesus' words about the little children: "Let them COME to me." (Mt 19:14) Remember Jesus' parable about the big dinner that had been prepared. The king sends word: "COME to the feast." (Mt 22:4) In the 4th Gospel, coming to Jesus means believing in Him. Thus Jesus says: "No one can COME to me unless the Father who sent me draws him." (In 6:44) In the majestic judgment picture which Matthew draws, there are those glorious words: "COME, you that are blessed by my Father, inherit the kingdom prepared for you."(Mt 25:34)

The word "COME' is the most beautiful word in the Bible, because it expresses a very deep theology. So very often it expresses the Grace of God calling us to union with God in Jesus Christ. And what the word "COME" makes clear to us is that God's Grace, God's Love, is not something we have to earn. It is always there waiting for us. All we have to do is COME. Come to the feast. Come, inherit the kingdom already prepared for you. God does not wait for us to see whether or not we shall take the journey toward God. No, God calls out to us: "COME."

And if the word "COME" is beautiful on the lips of the Lord Jesus, it is also beautiful on the lips of the Church. The New Testament ends with the vibrant cry of the Church: COME, Lord Jesus, COME!

May we not give play to our imaginations and ask ourselves about those last hours when Sr. Margaret Teresa remained in a coma. She was unable to speak or to be recognized by us, but may we not think that there was surely an inner conversation going on, that she was saying: "COME, Lord Jesus, COME!" And there was the reply:

"Arise my beloved, my beautiful one, and COME!
For see, the winter is past; the rains are over and gone.
Arise, my beloved, my beautiful one, and COME!
COME to the place prepared for you."

JEANNNE MALONE LOUGHERY 5-4-1996

THE SONG OF THE LARK

No program available

Jeanne Malone Loughery has died. A great actress has gone home to God. Jeanne was a great actress all her life. When I call her a great actress, I am not referring to the plays she took part in with Blackfriars or the plays she directed at Nazareth College. Neither am I referring to the false rumor that she had played a role in "Gang Busters." (Actually, she did have a part for a while in a radio show that at least a few of us here will remember:: "The New York State Troopers.")

When I say she was an actress all her life, I would not want to be misunderstood. I am not in any way suggesting that in her life she was play-acting. No, Jeanne was always real, always herself. She faced life earnestly and with joy. But in her speech, in her walk, in her gestures, it was so natural for her to be an actress.

There was a quality of soft and gentle beauty in her speech. When she walked it was with a special grace, almost as if she were gliding a couple of inches off the ground. And there was a charm and eloquence in her gestures. She could say more with her hands and her facial expressions than most of us can say in words. She could dismiss irrelevant problems with a motion of her hand. She could comfort the sorrowing with an encircling arm. She could capture hearts with a winsome smile.

She was beauty in motion. At times people who saw her wondered was she real or was she acting. She seemed too good to be true. Those of us who knew her well (and no one knew her better than her husband, Jim) knew that it was all real. It was herself. It was the way God made her. For this charm, grace, beauty was not just on the surface. It was an expression of something very deep inside: that spark of divinity in her that shone through in what she said and what she did. It was God's love manifested in her person: a love for God, for people and for God's good creation. A love that reached out to all who needed her. No wonder one of her favorite verses of poetry was from Edna St. Vincent Millay: "0 world, I cannot hold thee close enough."

Perhaps in a special way these words apply to the world of Nazareth College. For more than 35 years--from her matriculation at Nazareth in 1937 to her appointment as president in 1960 to her resignation from that office twelve years later, in 1972 -- Nazareth was the world to whom she said: "0 world, I cannot hold thee close enough." She became a faculty member at Nazareth in 1943 in the English Department and then in Speech and Drama.

Nor should I forget to mention that as a sister member of the faculty she took her turn exercising the unique and no longer existing ministry of "Dorm Sister." The "Dorm Sisters" were the unsung heroines of Nazareth's history. They deserve a special place in heaven, right next to the martyrs. These sisters, who lived with the students in the dormitories, formed a whole generation of students in love and loyalty to the college that probably could not be duplicated today. Without relinquishing any of their duties as religious, they took on, in addition, the role of mothers and fathers, doctors and nurses. They were counselors in moments of pain and in times of that terrible youthful affliction: boyfriend alienation. They held quivering hands and wiped away tears of distress. They were fashion critics at times of proms and other social events. They never knew at what time of day or night their ministries would be in demand. I have a theory, which I think is demonstrable from facts, that students seldom develop crucial problems until after midnight. The "Dorm Sisters" kept many a student from falling apart. Many alumnae still have their lives together, in no small measure due to the influence of the sisters who lived with them in the dorms.

In 1960 Jeanne would no longer be in the dormitories. The summer of that year she was called upon to inaugurate a new era in the history of Nazareth College. She was the first sister who was not the Superior of the Order to be appointed as president. She had little administrative experience to prepare her for the position, but she had the kind of gifts needed for the office. She met people easily and became well known in the community. In 1964 Henry Clune interviewed her. He was moved (I quote him) by "her grace, her charm, her liberality, her Christian spirit which shines through her eyes and informs her speech." "It is a privilege," he concluded his article, "in these days of chaos, vulgarity, bad manners, and disenchantment to meet someone with the Christian gentility of this great lady of Nazareth College" (Sunday D&C, June 21, 1964). He also mentioned in this article that "a pleasant lady brought us glasses of iced grape-juice and a plate of cookies." He recalled Jean remarking: "I'm sorry it isn't stronger."

Under Jeanne's leadership, Nazareth became a different college. The student body grew and became much more cosmopolitan. It was no longer a largely Monroe County school. Students came from far and wide. A much larger faculty was needed and were called to take a bigger role in the day-to-day life of the college. While her administrative duties were taxing, Jeanne always remained close to the students.

And the 1960s were difficult years in which to be president of a college. In 1965 a group of girls were grousing about things students usually groused about: the food, the rules, the professors, the grades. One of the girls suggested: "Let's draw up a list of all our grievances and march in front of the president's office and demand our rights." They began excitedly talking about making posters and what they would put on them. But then one of the wiser ones among them said: "You know what's going to happen? We going to march and shout our way across the campus and pound on her door. She will come out all smiling and ask: 'What can I do for you lovely girls today?' And we'll all sit down and cry." Thus abruptly ended the great student revolt at Nazareth.

I do remember another day that was a bit different. We were in the thick of the war in Viet Nam. Many of the girls had boyfriends who were there. There was much concern and debate about the morality of the war. One day, the president of student council, Stephanie Sullivan, came to Jeanne one day and told her (didn't ask her, but told her): "Tomorrow we are calling off classes. We are going to discuss the war in Viet Nam." Jeanne knew it was the time to acquiesce. And the next day there were discussions. The students took them seriously. Jeanne knew instinctively that this would be an important, if painful, moment in Nazareth's history.

The students knew that Jeanne loved them, and loved them too much to let them get away with anything but their best: academically, socially, spiritually. She knew theirs were minds that need to be opened to explore the truth and hearts that needed to be opened to reach the good and the beautiful.

Jeanne was a lot of fun to be with. There was a secret she and I shared between us. It grew out of the frequent visits that Bishop Kearney used to make to the campus. Bishop Kearney always smelled nice when he came. On one occasion after he had left Jeanne said to me: "You know, he wears Chanel No. 5." I said to her: "Do you think it's time for me to do the same?" "Oh, no," she said, "Not yet. I'll tell you when it's time." That was our little secret. Every once in a while I would ask her: "Is it time yet?" She would always shake her head and say: "Not yet." Now I shall never know when the time has come. Or maybe I shall experience a whiff of perfume fall from out the sky some day as a kind of heavenly sign telling me: "The time has come. Out with the Chanel No. 5."

When Jeanne left the presidency of Nazareth College in 1972, she came to see that God was calling her to an new and unexpected vocation. She married the man she had come to love. Their life together and their concern for one another have been an example of Christian married love to many. There were times of hardship and suffering during the more than 20 years of their life together, but, as Jim has said, they were beautiful, exquisite years deeply prized by both of them. Now she has gone to God, where she will look out for Jim in another way. We pray that he may find an inner peace that somehow will compensate in some small measure at least for her physical absence from his life.

And now we all give her back to God from whom she came. And as we do so, I think of one of the plays that was performed at Nazareth under her direction or at least under her watchful eye. The play was Jean Anouilh's "The Lark." It's a play about one of Jeanne's favorite persons, Joan of Arc. Toward the end of the play Cauchon, the Bishop of Beauvais, who presided at her trial, says in effect: "History will not remember us, but her story will survive, and it will be a story of joy. She is the lark singing in the open sky."

Jeanne was a free spirit. Not even suffering could contain her. Her life was indeed a story of joy. We shall remember her. In our hearts and maybe — in some special moments — in the open sky, we shall continue to hear the "song of the lark."

SR. KATHRYN SULLIVAN 5-6-1996

Readings: Wisdom 6: 12-16
Revelation 21: 1-7
John 4: 5-15

A woman comes to the well. She meets a Stranger weary from his journey. The woman was weary too – weary of life and its endless routine of meaninglessness. But at that moment at the well, Wisdom graciously appeared to her. Jesus made her look into the well. Not the well from which every day she had come to draw water, but the well that was inside her that no one had ever helped her to see. In that inner well she saw her real self for the first time. Life took on meaning, and there was joy in her heart.

I shall return to the well in a moment. But first I want to say that, in many ways, Sr. Kathryn was a formidable person. She was a woman of grace and charm and dignity, too. She may have been small in stature, especially in these last years. But she had an impressive mind and a clear vision and a strong will. I have to own up to the fact that, while I loved her and respected her, I was always a bit intimidated by her. When she made suggestions to me, like the suggestion she was constantly making – that I teach a course in Church history – I seemed to revert to an earlier stage of development and stood at attention and answered: "Yes, Sister." There was one time, years ago, that I thought she would be pleased, because I had team-taught a course on Church history and art with Sr. Magdalen. "Oh, no," she said, "what we need is a whole course on Church history." Again I stood at attention and said: "Yes, Sister." And I hope that she isn't angry with me that I never did do that course.

There is a passage in the book of Numbers (Chapter 13), where Moses sends spies to reconnoiter the land God had given to his people. They return from their expedition and report about the people of that land: "They are all giants." I think this may express something of the feeling we all have had in these past few days with Sister Kathryn dying just after Jeanne Malone Loughery had gone to God: "They were giants." And now they are gone. It's somewhat like the feeling that those of us, who have been with the college many years experienced when Srs. Teresa Marie, Agnes Patricia, Raphael, Rose Miriam and Rose Marie died. We thought to ourselves at the time: "The giants are gone."

But always a loving providence raises up new leaders. Jeanne and Kathryn became the giants, the leaders, who would shape a new generation in the story of Nazareth. Like Romulus and Remus, like Peter and Paul, they worked together to found a "new" Nazareth. It was a new Nazareth, yet not a Nazareth that was cut off from its roots and its earliest traditions.

Perhaps it would be truer to say it was a maturing Nazareth. Jeane and Kathryn inserted their stories into something greater than either of them, namely, the Great Story of Nazareth College. By the Great Story I mean the on-going, ever growing, yet unbroken Tradition of a collegial community, as it has moved from its foundation in 1924 to the present reality that it is today.

Who of the founding sisters would have thought that just this past week, as two great leaders of Nazareth were returning to God, the college they loved would be launching a ten million dollar drive? Much less could they have even dreamed that our local paper, which a few generations ago hardly even knew we existed, has endorsed this drive and urged the people of Rochester to get involved, because Nazareth has contributed so much to the Rochester community.

The founding sisters might not recognize the campus as it looks today, but they would recognize the Great Story, the Great Tradition that continues to be there and continues to grow as Nazareth endeavors to meet the needs of her students in new and changing times.

Jeanne and Kathryn each contributed their significant stories to the Great Story of which we all in some way form a part. I would dare say that the contribution that Sr. Kathryn made might be summed up in a single word. She was a woman of culture. An avid reader, she drank deeply from the well of good literature, poetry, fiction, and literary essays. And like any truly educated person she had an eager enthusiasm for good literate mystery stories.

I might add – she was my first publisher. Surely a sign of her good taste. Years ago, when the student body was small enough that faculty and students could gather in the old auditorium, we had an annual college convocation on Founders' Day. Faculty and students attended in academic attire. In 1960 Fr. Benedict Ehmann was invited to give an address on John Henry Newman. It was a fine talk and at the gathering after the talk, in what we used to call "the Bishop's Parlor," I said to Sr. Kathryn: "There were two things Newman wanted very much to do, but was not allowed. First, he wanted to make a fresh translation of the Bible into English; and second, he wanted to return to Oxford as Catholic chaplain. Both these undertakings (which were not allowed to Newman) were later carried out by Ronald Knox. So I think it would be appropriate next year to have the Founders' Day address on Ronald Knox." "Yes," she said, "and you are the one to give it." Again I reverted to my grade school posture and said very quickly: "Yes, Sister." I gave the talk in 1961. Sr. Kathryn had the talk printed and thus became my first publisher.

As dean, Kathryn was deeply interested in both the students and their teachers. For she believed that the young people who came to Nazareth came with minds that needed to be enlightened and made free. She also believed that they deserved a faculty that could turn them on to the excitement of learning, to the joy of searching for truth: not a truth that would simply be handed to them, but a truth they must struggle for and make their own. She was a woman of taste and refinement. She had dug deeply into the well of knowledge herself and was convinced that it was the task of the college to bring young students to that well so that they, too, might drink from it in abundance.

I use the analogy of the well to describe Sr. Kathryn and the goal she would set for the Nazareth College community, because Sr. Jamesetta told me of Kathryn's interest in wells. It began when they were in Israel and on the day she and Kathryn visited Jacob's well at Shechem, where Jesus conversed with the Samaritan woman. Kathryn was deeply impressed by the well and told Jamesetta that from then on the story of the Samaritan woman would have a very special meaning for her. She had chosen that story as the reading for her jubilee and it seemed most fitting to use it for her funeral.

Sacred wells have played a large part in human history. Thomas Merton has written that "men [and women] instinctively regard themselves as wanderers and wayfarers and it is second nature for them to go on pilgrimage in search of a privileged and holy place, a center and source of indefectible life." And oftentimes the place the pilgrimage led to was a holy well. Going to the holy well was a symbol of the inner journey to the source of living waters. There are holy wells throughout the Holy Land, holy wells through Europe, and Ireland is full of them.

Wells are not necessarily stagnant waters; often they are underground springs of pure, clean water. The well, therefore, is an apt symbol of freshness and new life, a symbol of coming alive in a new way. And that coming alive in a new way is what education meant to Kathryn. To become educated is to drink deeply of the well-springs of knowledge, human and divine. To become educated is to find that well deep within oneself and to plumb its depths., as did the Samaritan woman, and so discover our own true reality.

As dean of Nazareth College, Kathryn knew that the students of Nazareth needed to work for a number of goals. They had to learn how to make a living and she believed in that. But, more significantly, she believed they had to make a life. It was important that they learn information; more important that they acquire knowledge; most important that they achieve wisdom.

Information is simply raw, unconnected data. When information is organized into some kind of meaningful whole or pattern we may speak of it as knowledge. Wisdom is knowledge of reality taken back to its Source. Wisdom is grasping or being grasped by the Real in all that is real. By the Real (with a capital 'r') I mean that which alone is Real in itself and is therefore the Real in everything that is real.

A college deals with knowledge. Some knowledge is closer to information; other knowledge is closer to wisdom. It is the second kind of knowledge that especially builds and enhances the human spirit. Sr. Kathryn would have applauded the words of Ralph Waldo Emerson: "Raphael paints wisdom. Handel sings it, Shakespeare writes it. Wren builds it."

The book of Proverbs speaks of Wisdom as mixing her wine and preparing her table. Jeanne and Kathryn, the two towering figures of Nazareth's recent past, made sure that Wisdom's table was set at Nazareth and that students were invited to partake of her splendid fare. It is that table – wisdom's table – that is at the heart of the Great Story of Nazareth.

Sr. Kathryn, as we give you back to the Stranger you met at the well in your own life, many thanks. Many thanks for having made a difference at Nazareth College. Many thanks for the life and talent you gave so generously. And... let me say... I'm no longer scared of you!

SR. GABRIELLA MALONEY 11-7-1996

Readings: Isaiah 25:6, 7-9
Revelation 14: 1-5
Matthew 25: 14-21

When we tell the story of the Christian community, we begin with the apostolic age: those who were with Jesus at the beginning. Gradually they died and a second generation – post-apostolic age – took their places. These second generation Christians were very important: first because they were in touch with the church's founders; and second, because, building on the apostolic foundations, they were the ones who gave the direction that the Christian community would take as it moved into an unknown and ever expanding future.

There is something of a parallel to the Church's beginnings and growth in the Nazareth story. The founders of Nazareth College have all gone to God. They began a story which they handed on to a second generation of leaders. We are here tonight because yet another one of those second generation leaders of the college has joined those founders and bequeathed the continuing growth of the Nazareth story to others. The Nazareth that Sr. Gabriella helped to lead was different from the Nazareth of the founders. And the Nazareth of today is light-years removed from the Nazareth of which Sr. Gabriella was so important a part.

Yet, while so many things are different, there is a continuity. It is to be found in the Great Story that takes into itself the particular stories of the 70 some years of Nazareth's existence. For the Great Story is the tradition of Nazareth College. Rooted in the vision and wisdom of the past, it is yet living and ever young, with something peculiarly new and original to say to people of today. That Tradition, which is the Big Story, is something always old and yet ever new, because it is always being revivified. It is born again in each generation of Nazareth folk, to be lived and applied in new and particular ways. This Big Story, the Tradition, teaches us – faculty, administrators, students, friends – how to live, because it develops and expands our powers of mind and heart, spirit and faith. It also shows us how to offer ourselves as a leaven in our culture and a challenge to a life of valor and greatness to the world in which we live.

Sr. Gabriella made a contribution to Nazareth's story that can never quite be matched. We choose the Gospel of the talents deliberately as appropriate for one aspect of her gift of herself to the college. We usually think of talents as skills or gifts that a person has; actually, the talent was a piece of money. In fact, it was the largest denomination of money known in Jesus' day. It is difficult to say how much it was; but it has been estimated to be an amount that would give a worker an ordinary day's pay for 16 years. So a talent is a huge amount of money.

I think Sr. Gabriella would probably include in herself all three of the servants mentioned in the Gospel and entrusted with such huge amounts of money. She would certainly double the five and double the two. And I can imagine that she may also have had hidden a smaller fund to take care of unforeseen problems that might arise. In fact, a faculty member told me the charming story of how she was once asked where the money would come for a particular improvement that had to be made. Her answer: "I put away a little here, a little there, and then I have faith that we will have what we need."

Yes, she was indeed a whiz with money. She knew how to make it grow. Who do you think taught Steve LaSalle all the things that make him such a good vice-president for financial affairs?

In fact, I would say that Sr. Gabriella is the only person I know who, from her own experience, could speak directly to Jesus, look him straight in the eyes and tell him that he was wrong. There is a saying of Jesus, which can be found in both Matthew's Gospel and Luke's (Mt. 6:24; Lk. 16:14), which warns us: "You cannot serve God and money." Sr. Gabriella could say back to him what the fellow on the TV ad used to say: "O yes, you can." She served her college well in finances, but she also served her God with deep love and commitment. Conclusion: she served God and money. And I wouldn't be at all surprised that she might at this very moment be telling Jesus that he should be more careful about making such sweeping generalizations.

Yet, while we marvel at her amazing competence in dealing with financial affairs, I would be woefully amiss if I seemed to suggest that her principal interest was in money. She was interested in the college. The college was a family for her. The only value the money had to her was that it helped that family to remain healthy and to grow.

She was one of that unique group of sisters who took her turn living in the dorms. I remember the time that Lourdes Hall was being built. To make room for the overflow of students, the front part of the basement of Smyth Hall was turned into a dormitory; and Sr. Gabriella was the Dorm sister in that unusual dorm. The students used as a kind of community room what used to be called the "day-hop" lounge. My office was just above that room. I remember a number of evenings when Sr. Gabriella would send one of the students to my office and invite me to join them in a snack of cookies and hot chocolate. [I expect that the evenings I was invited the girls were given orders as to how they should be attired]. I have often recalled that beautiful experience of family that Sr. Gabriella helped to create among those young women and, indeed, in the rest of the college.

Next to God, the college was her consuming interest. And though she was able to serve God and money, she never forgot which came first. She never lost sight of her commitment as a religious to find God in her own life and to help others do the same in theirs.

Sr. Gabriella died in November, the month we traditionally think of as the month of the holy souls. I wish we would change the name of this month and call it the month of the communion of saints. Our beloved dead are not just souls; they are persons who see the face of God. If they experience Purgatory, it is – so it seems to me – a moment of immediate purification that takes place when they first see God. At that moment, which is perhaps the very moment of death, they are purified of all that is not of God and enter into the bliss of the 144,000 mentioned in the book of Revelation. Of course that number is not really a number; it's a way of saying countless saints happy in the presence of God

When we think of the communion of saints we need to think of ourselves: we are saints in the making, for our lives have been transformed by participation in the death and resurrection of Jesus. We share communion with one another: that is the earthly communion of saints. But there is a thin veil -- thinner than we think – between us and those who have transcended the boundaries of death. They are models for us and intercessors. But I think, most of all, they are a challenge to us: a challenge to become aware of what really matters in life. More than that they are a challenge to us in that they have left unfinished business which they bequeath to us. For example, Oscar Romero began a ministry of justice and peace and service to the oppressed people of his country. His bequest to us is to carry on that work.

So, too, Sr. Gabriella and all the other college people who have gone to God bequeath to us the Tradition of Nazareth College. They challenge us to continue the Great Story which they began. Commemorating the saints, as we do this month, means accepting that challenge. It means that we are willing to follow in their footsteps and build on the tradition they have handed over to us. Our call is to continue to grow eagerly and courageously into an exciting future that is ahead of us: the future of a new century and a new millennium.

Sr. Louise Weber 3-3-2006

Eph. 3: 14-22
Phil. 3:7:14
Jn. 15: 9-17

We gather here to celebrate the life of Sr. Louise Weber: a life rich with the many graces God extended to her, a life rich in the many ways in which she made herself a gift to others. As I reflected on the readings for this Mass, I was struck by their beauty and appropriateness. Louise chose the readings for this Mass. I don't know when she chose them. But, whenever it was, I can only say that they were chosen with a singularly prophetic insight. Let's take a quick look at them and see how remarkably they fit together.

The Gospel may be read as Jesus' gift of himself to Louise. It includes his call to her to abide, to live, in his love. But this call to abide in him includes a promise: the promise of intimate friendship as Jesus says to her: I don't think of you any longer as my servants, but as my friends, with all the rights and privileges that accompany friendship.

If the Gospel is Jesus' gift to Louise, the reading from *Philippians* may be read as her gift of herself to Jesus. It is a gift of everything. Nothing is held back. How amazingly prophetic the words: "I have accepted the loss of all things." We have all seen how completely and totally she had, in these last years, let go of all that we might rightly think of as important in human life. She tells us in this reading that she is ready to see it all as rubbish, if through suffering she can come to share in the power of the resurrection.

If the Gospel may be read as Jesus' gift to her and the reading from *Philippians* as her gift to Jesus, we may well see the reading from *Ephesians* as her gift to us. She prays that Christ may dwell in our hearts and that, through faith rooted in love, we may come to know the breadth, height, length, depth of Jesus' love for us, and that we may be filled with the fullness of God.

To sum it all up, we might say that the Gospel is theology: God's gift to Louise. The *Philippian* reading is autobiography: Louise's gift of herself to God. And the *Ephesian* reading is spirituality: her gift of spiritual counsel for all of us.

It is in the glow of these amazing readings that we gather to celebrate the richness of the life that Sr. Louise Weber lived among us. A graduate of Nazareth College, a well respected teacher, registrar, dorm mother, director of the alumnae association, she was "Joe Louis" to students and alumnae who loved her for her genuine concern for them and her ready willingness to help them in whatever ways she could. She was a topflight organizer. Sr. Jamesetta said the other day: "Louse could organize an army if she were asked to do so." Then, of course, there were her many achievements in the congregation: as member of the Central Administration, and long time as treasurer and as adviser to so many sisters whose lives and ministry she helped to shape.

A gracious, loving woman who spread good cheer and goodness wherever she went: this is the Louise we all remember. This is the Louise we want to celebrate today in this liturgy.

But we all know that there was another side to her story: those last years of her life that were such a mystery to us, as we watched this loving, vibrant, outgoing woman drifting away from us and seeming to be entering into an interior world that we simply could not reach. The question I want to ask is this: Can we celebrate today this part of her story – those last years -- or do we simply leave those years untouched as something we can never even begin to comprehend?

Sixty-four years ago, Louise became a Sister of St. Joseph. She knelt before an altar and, not knowing what the future held for her, she professed her desire to give her whole life to God in the congregation of the Sisters of St. Joseph. I want to invite you -- in the light of her life's story as we know it -- to reflect imaginatively about what God may have said to her that day about the future course her life would take -- though it would only be through the living out of her life in the congregation that finally, over the years, she would be able to hear all that God said to her at that time. Thus, for most of her lifetime, those final years would have remained hidden from her.

Here is one way of imagining what God may have said to her:

"Louise, as you begin your life as a dedicated Sister of St. Joseph, I am going to give you gifts that will endear you to many people. You will have the gift of a gracious hospitality that will welcome all those who come into your life. You will leave your imprint on Nazareth College, where you will be loved and honored by students, faculty and alumnae. You will exercise leadership among the Sisters of St. Joseph. The example of your life will be a source of inspiration to many sisters who will see you as a shining example of the kind of person a Sister of St. Joseph should be.

"But then [and this is the part she would have heard not earlier, but only as it happened] after you have achieved much and worked so much and been so widely praised, I shall begin to take your gifts away from you. I will take away your health and your strength and your lucidity. I will call you to enter into my passion.

"I will lead you along a lonely and fearful path, where no one will be able to follow you. I will draw you into a darkness that no one will understand, that you will not even understand yourself. You will appear as if abandoned and rejected. Your friends will shake their heads and grieve for you.

"You must not be afraid to taste the anguish and the poverty of the darkness into which I shall be bringing you. For, whether you understand fully or not, I will be at your side in the midst of it all. In ways that will never be grasped by those who stand and pray at your bedside, you will experience my presence.

"Through your sufferings, I shall do great good for many people. Do not ask me how I shall do this or why I do it. For you will not yet be able to understand.

"And after you have suffered much – more than you thought you could endure – the Third Day will come. And I shall raise you up into the heights of my Joy. You shall die into me; and in my mercy you shall find once again all that you seem to have lost – and so much more shall you find than you could ever have imagined. Only then shall you begin to see why I chose to lead you along the way of suffering and darkness.

"Today the power of the resurrection stirs within you. Arise, my beloved, and come. For, see, the winter is passed for you. The rains are over. The song of the dove is heard in the land. Arise, my beloved, my beautiful one, and come."

Yes, I believe that we can celebrate these last difficult years. We can celebrate not only the fact that they are over, but that, in some mysterious way that we cannot yet comprehend, they are an integral part of God's involvement in the fullness of Louise's story. That fullness that leads to resurrection. It is the Third Day of her life.

SR. MARY FRANCIS NORMAN 10-3-1988

Readings: Ezekiel 36: 24-28
1 Peter 4: 7-11
John 15: 9-17

     While Sr. Mary Francis was not at Nazareth College from its earliest beginnings, she became a member of the faculty close enough to that beginning that she was surely one of those who helped forge the spirit that became Nazareth College; and, therefore, can at least in an unofficial way be listed among the founders. She was already on the faculty when the college moved to its present location. She took over the leadership of the Music

Department at a critical moment in that department's history and gave it a direction and a sense of stability and identity that it very much needed at the time. She was a competent teacher and a strong administrator. In fact, I would venture the word "strong" as an accurate term to describe her; not only as an administrator, but as a person. She showed a strength that came from a deep and calm sense of knowing what she was doing and why. She had a sense of purpose in life and a deep commitment to mission.

I did not know her so much as a music teacher. My talents do not run in the field of music; in fact, some of my friends think they run in the opposite direction. I knew Sr. Mary Francis as one of many sisters at the college who exercised that unique and no longer existing ministry of "Dorm Sister." There must surely be a special place in heaven for such sisters. Probably right next to the martyrs. These sisters, who lived in the dormitories, are the unsung heroines of Nazareth College's history. They formed a whole generation of students in a love and loyalty to the college that probably could not be duplicated today— certainly not in the same way and, quite probably, not at the same depth.

These sisters engaged in multiple ministries. Now there is nothing especially unusual in engaging in multiple ministries. Indeed, it is becoming a common thing in religious communities for a sister who has worked a certain amount of time in a particular ministry to turn to another ministry. This can be very helpful for her own growth. And in the course of a lifetime in religion there may be sisters who will have exercised multiple ministries.

The difference between those sisters and the "Dorm Sisters" is that they exercise these different ministries *successively* and often with some time of transition in between. The "Dorm Sisters", on the other hand, exercised multiple ministries *simultaneously*. Without relinquishing any of their responsibilities as religious, they were mothers and fathers, doctors and nurses. They were counselors in moments of pain and boy-friend alienation. They held quivering hands and wiped away tears of distress. They were fashion-critics at times of proms and other social events: from the Blue Danube Ball to the Junior Prom and so many others besides. And they were never quite sure at what time of the day or night they would be called upon to exercise a particular ministry. I have a theory that I think is demonstrable that students seldom develop critical problems until after midnight. The "Dorm Sisters" kept many a student from falling apart. Many alumnae still have their lives together, in no small measure due to the influence of the sisters who lived with them in the dorms.

It was in this kind of selfless capacity that I chiefly came to know Sr. Mary Francis. If I were to describe what she did for the resident students she lived with, I guess I would want to say that she was a good disciplinarian. But, in the very act of saying this, I want to give a very particular meaning to disciplinarian. A disciplinarian, in the literal sense of that word, is not just a person who keeps order and makes sure that everyone toes the mark. The word discipline derives from the Latin word *discens*, which means "to teach" Sr. Mary Francis was a teacher, not just of music theory and music history; she was a teacher of young women. She taught them how to live and how to grow up. She taught them to assume responsibility. She had the rare gift of understanding young people and their needs, and not the least their need and even their desire for a proper discipline. The students knew that she loved them; and loved them too much to let them get away with anything but their best: academically, socially and spiritually. She knew theirs were minds that needed to be opened to the truth and hearts that needed to be open to good. Education should do something similar to what

Ezekiel speaks of: giving people new minds and new hearts, helping them to become the new creations that they were called to be.

I said that she was a good disciplinarian. She could be a "tough" one at times too. She taught for keeps. There was no nonsense, no fooling around, where essentials were concerned. But I would be false to her true image, if I did not add that she was tough with a twinkle in her eye. I never saw her laugh very much, though I am sure she did. But I do remember the roguish smile that could light up her face, that sometimes had to be concealed, with difficulty, when some "little villain" (as she sometimes affectionately called her charges) got out of order and had to be called in on the carpet. However much they may have resented the discipline at the moment, they knew, with the sure instinct that young people have, that it was a discipline that came from the heart and was aimed at their own hearts.

And in the long run, they became her friends. So many of them remembered her and visited her after their graduation. And their loyalty to her was not only an affection for her, but a commitment to what she stood for. And what she stood for was the Gospel. I said she was a disciplinarian. The word is closely linked with the word "disciple". Indeed, one way in which a disciplinarian might be defined is "a person who makes disciples" Mary Francis made disciples – not disciples committed to her, but disciples devoted, each in her own way, to the God whom she served and to whom they knew she had given her life in its totality. She returns that life to God in all its richness. She has entered into the fullness of friendship with Him who long ago no longer called her servant, but friend. For He made known to her what he had learned from the Father and through her he produced abundant fruit: fruit that shall remain -- in the hearts of many people.

SR. MARY LOURDES MacCARTHY 7-6-1996

Readings: Micah 6: 6-8
1 Corinthians 13: 1-13
Luke 2: 25-32

The year 1958 will always be a memorable year in the life of the Roman Catholic Church and in the life of Nazareth College. For the Church, it was the year in which Giuseppe Roncalli became Pope John XXIII and instituted a reform that would change the face of the Roman Catholic Church. For Nazareth College, 1958 was the year that

Sister Mary Lourdes MacCarthy arrived at Nazareth. The Nazareth she came to was on the verge of dramatic changes that would propel it into the life of the contemporary world. And Mary Lourdes was to play a significant role in helping to build a new and better Nazareth.

Almost from the beginning of our working together (and when she came she augmented the Religion Department by 100% - from 1 to 2) I saw in her the wonderful capacity for change and a fearlessness about embarking upon it, too. When she saw that change was needed to make the Gospel more appealing and Nazareth more exciting and attractive academically, she was willing to move, no matter what the cost. And there were times in those early years when the costs were high, when we were misunderstood and had to struggle to win acceptance and approval for the direction in which we both knew we had to move as a department. And while we may have been misunderstood, there were no misunderstandings between us. We worked together as colleagues in harmony and friendship.

And for that friendship I shall always be grateful. I shall also be grateful for all that I learned from her and the goodness I experienced in her and from her. Her personality was always warm and welcoming. You knew she loved people. Most accepting of everyone and anyone, her heart went out especially to those who were most needy. She had special gifts as a teacher and she was never afraid to try out new ideas and move in new directions. I mentioned to the Motherhouse sisters the day after she died that I once asked her: "Mary Lourdes, are you sometimes surprised at the things you find yourself saying?" "Surprised?" she answered, "I'm shocked." She had a mind that was open to new ideas and a heart that was open to all.

Yet, I must say that, as much as I loved her (and I did), I never felt that I fully knew her or understood her. There was a mystery about her that one never quite reached, so it seemed to me at least. I suppose that, in a sense, this is true of every person, but it seemed especially true of her. There was a depth in her that she shared perhaps only with God. It was not that she was trying to hide herself from others. On the contrary, she welcomed so many into her life with great openness and charm. But there was that something of God in her that she could share only with the Hidden Ground of Love in whom she lived and had her being.

Indeed it was this mystery about her, I believe, that was very much a part of the charm of her person. You came away from being with her with the feeling: I am happy and delighted in the knowledge and love I have of her; yet I know there is so much more there. She was mystery as God is mystery: not mystery that repels, but mystery that attracts. And now she is one with the great Mystery of God.

I want to say a word to Norma and Josepha and all the people at 4141 East Avenue and all those who were close to Sr. Mary Lourdes. I want to say what Brother Maurice Flood said of Thomas Merton in the Merton documentary. That documentary closes with a picture of Brother Maurice looking straight into the camera and saying very simply of Thomas Merton: "He is still with us. He lives in our hearts." I want to say to all of you: we believe in the communion of saints. What does this mean? It means we believe that between us and those who have died into new and immortal life, there is a thin veil, often and, perhaps more easily than we think, brushed aside. Yes, I want to say to all of you who loved her so dearly: she has gone to God, but she has not left you. She is still with you. This is not an empty bit of sweet piety. It is good theology.

There is a wonderful poem by R. S. Thomas called "The Morrow." It's about the day after the funeral of a loved one. He describes a period of weeping, then one of reflection, and finally a moment of deep insight.

> That day after the night death;
> That night after the day's wailing,
> I went out on the hill
>> And contemplated the lit windows
>> and the stars, those flocks
>> without a shepherd; and I asked:
>> "Is she up there, the woman
>> who was the pawn that love
>> offered in exchange for beauty?"
>> Later I was alone in my room
>> reading and, the door (being) closed,
>> she was there, speechlessly enquiring:
>> Was all well? It was true
>> what the book said in answer
>> to the world's question as to where
>> at death does the soul go:
>> "There is no need under a pillarless
>> heaven for it to go anywhere."

Yes, she is with you. She is still a presence in your lives, at your side, speechlessly enquiring: "Are you all right? Is all well?" Believe in that presence, for it is true, ever so gloriously true.

SR. MARY GERARD FLAGLER 12-18-1995

Readings: Is. 25: 1-10
Song of Songs 2: 8-14
Lk. 1: 39-56

Well, Mary Gerard, this time you made it. To Jerusalem. The heavenly Jerusalem, that is. As you enter into the joys of the new and everlasting Jerusalem, I am sure you cannot help but think of the abortive attempt you made to enter into the earthly Jerusalem. And if there should be (God forbid) any hospitals in the heavenly Jerusalem, I am sure you are giving them a wide berth.

Our first reading is about the exiles from Babylon who returned to the earthly Jerusalem. The prophet offers them all sorts of promises. A holy way will be built through the desert. The desert will blossom with wonderful flowers and flow with fresh streams. With the prophet's glorious promises ringing in their hearts, the exiles journeyed to Jerusalem with great expectations only to be disappointed when they got there and found everything in ruins. There expectation went largely unfulfilled.

I remember fourteen years ago, Mary Gerard, the day we flew out of Rochester, then across the Atlantic, finally arriving at Ben Gurion airport, whence we went by bus to our Jerusalem hotel. As we approached the Holy City we sang the song that pilgrims sang centuries ago as they went up with joy to the Holy City, the song that was our psalm response in this liturgy. You were filled with great expectations and anticipations. After years of teaching in various places (including teaching my brother at Aquinas) you were at last on your way to the place you had always dreamed of visiting: to the land where Jesus had lived. You looked forward with anticipatory delight to visiting all the holy places graced by Jesus' presence. Like the exiles who came from Babylon centuries ago, you looked forward to a glorious experience of Jerusalem.

And what happened? You didn't fare much better than the exiles from Babylon. On the very first day you landed in the cardiac intensive care unit at the Hadassah hospital which is just outside the city of Jerusalem! I heard of your heart attack when I was with our group making the stations. We were at the Fourth Station. I got a taxi and dashed to the hospital. I found you sitting up, quite alert, and quite resigned to the doctor's diagnosis that, while you would recover, you would be in hospital at least two weeks and then would have to rest for at least another two weeks.

To be sure, you can't see much of the Holy Land from the cardiac unit of the Hadassah hospital nor from the four-bed ward you were moved to later from the cardiac unit. Remember that four-bed room that already had five beds in it? And the wide open windows that let in a bit of air in the hot summer: a bit of air and a lot of flies? I recall how, teacher that you were, you rated the hospital: the cardiac unit got an A+; the four-bed ward a reluctant C.

All the time you were in the hospital, I never saw you weep or heard you complain. I never heard you ask: why did this have to happen to me? That practical sense of living with reality as it is l that you always had did not desert you. I am not suggesting that it was easy. But you had faced tough situations before (after all, you had "broken in" quite a number of novices when you had the job of Motherhouse sacristan) . You knew how to deal with adversity and not lose your good humor. In fact, I remember one day you said to me, with that wry smile that spread over your whole face: "Well, I guess I'm unique. Very few people have this kind of experience of Jerusalem." Very few indeed.

Remember how, after you left the hospital, I was able to get rooms for you and Joan Margaret and myself at Ecce Homo, a delightful hostel run by the Sisters of Zion and built over the place where Pilate judged Jesus? We stayed there nearly two weeks before coming home. Remember how determined Joan Margaret and I were that you see something of Jerusalem before we left? We hired a taxi to give you a three-hour ride through Jerusalem. We had to walk a long distance to get to the taxi. Remember how I was scared (even though you weren't) that you might have another heart attack? And how we carried a chair along with us and made you sit down every ten feet till we got to the taxi? That was all you saw of the Holy Land you had come thousands of miles to visit.

I want to return to the Hadassah hospital for a moment (that hospital known for its excellent medical care and for the wonderful Chagall windows of the twelve tribes of Israel that grace the windows of the hospital chapel). Do you remember, Mary Gerard, how the first day you were there I told you about the location of the hospital? That it was built on an elevation overlooking the charming little village of Em Karim. Nestled in a lovely valley this town was the place to which Mary went. For this village was the home of Zachary and Elizabeth. Your hospital overlooked the place of the Visitation. Remember the days we celebrated Eucharist in the cardiac unit behind the closed curtains. (We are probably the only ones who ever celebrated Eucharist there.) And I left the Blessed Sacrament with you. The tiny cabinet next to your bed became a tabernacle. Wasn't it exciting to think that, just as Mary had brought Jesus to Em Karim, you brought Jesus to the Hadassah Hospital so very near to Fin Karim? I am sure that always remained a special remembrance for you and gave you a special kinship with Mary of the Visitation.

As I reflect on that trip to the Holy Land, I wonder who profited most from the visit there? The rest of us were dashing about trying to see everything, as tour groups usually do. We were in the land blessed by Jesus' presence. Yet we were in so much of a hurry to get to all the Holy Places that we could easily lose sight of what we were really experiencing. You, on the other hand, in your hospital bed had the time to realize that, even though you were hospitalized, you too were in the land made holy by Jesus' presence. You could take the time to revel in that experience.

Though Sr. Joan Margaret and I and others visited you, there were still many hours when you were alone. You had time to pray and reflect and to experience the tabernacled Jesus present with you. Yes, as I reflect, I think it was you who got the greatest profit from the trip to the Holy Land. The rest of us were there to see; in the mysterious designs of God, you were there simply to be. You did not see the places the rest of us saw, but in the depths of your solitude, I am sure God was very close to you: you heard the voice of the Beloved. Our God is a loving God, who would not leave you alone. The Beloved was standing behind every wall, gazing in at the windows, looking through the lattice. Yes, Mary Gerard, your experience was unique, not just because it was unusual, but because it was so deeply a time filled with all sorts of possibilities of grace.

On Wednesday your Beloved spoke to you and said:
Arise, my love, my fair one, and come away;
for now the winter is past,
the rain is over and gone.
The flowers appear
the time of singing has come.
Arise my love, my fair one, and come away. . .

Yes, Mary Gerard, you finally made it Jerusalem, to the true Jerusalem, of which the earthly Jerusalem is but a shadowy symbol: the heavenly Jerusalem, where there are no cardiac units, only the wondrous and inexplicable Presence of your Beloved, where you experience joy we cannot even imagine. Without really knowing what we mean, we say to you: ENJOY.

SR. MARGARET MARY TOWNSEND 1-21-1984

Hosea 2:16, 21-22
Philippians 1:27-28
Matthew 9:35-37, 10:1

The Gospel passage we have chosen for this liturgy is a picture of Jesus' compassion for the sick. He is the divine Physician or, if you will, the divine Nurse who is so moved at the sight of pain and suffering that He wills to use all the skills at His disposal to bring relief to people.

It should be noted that Jesus' concern is directed to the whole person. He not only cures them of sickness and disease; he also expels evil spirits – which is really to say that His healing touch extends to their inner selves as well as to their bodies. Jesus heals the whole person.

The Gospel is also about the first sending ceremony in which Jesus summons the Twelve and gives them authority to expel unclean spirits and to cure sickness and disease of every kind. And if the Twelve had been women – and there are those who believe this might have been a better choice – I suppose this might well have been the first capping ceremony in history. And Jesus' commission to the Twelve to cure people in both spirit and body could well be considered the first charge to practice holistic medicine.

During her years of teaching at Nazareth College, Sister Margaret Mary built the Nursing Department with a discipline that would have been the envy of a Marine drill sergeant, yet that discipline was tempered with a love and a tenderness which, try as she would, she could not quite conceal from her students. There was a transparency to her care and concern that all her gruffness and crustiness could not hide.

There is much talk in medicine today about patient advocacy. The task of such an advocate is to safeguard the rights and the personal dignity of the patient, to see that the patient does not get lost in the system, to assure that the patient has a name and is not just a number.

This issue is a difficult one, for patients being transitory are not readily able to organize and choose their advocates. Traditionally of course – long before special patient-advocates were talked about – nurses were looked upon as the ones who carried out this role.

In a sense, patient-advocacy is but one aspect of a serious need in our society: the need to defend the rights, the dignity and the uniqueness of persons. We live in a mass-society in which the media try to make us think alike and fashions try to make us look alike. There is real danger of the person being lost in the collectivity. In such a situation we need not only patient-advocates; we need person-advocates too.

At Christmas time I received a letter from Kay Weiman Sullivan, a graduate of the Nursing Department who now lives in Kansas City. She wrote, among other things, that she tells her students: "All I learned about student-person advocacy I learned from Sister Margaret Mary. She taught it and lived it."

There is much truth in Kay's tribute. Sister Margaret Mary not only taught person-advocacy to her students, she also practiced a deep personalism toward them. She knew every student in her department and almost everything about them. She knew what they were doing and when they misbehaved. She passed judgment on their dates and reviewed the candidates for their hands.

When, after their first year at Nazareth, she placed a cap on their heads – ably assisted by Bishop Kearney – she already knew each of these students in their uniqueness; in fact for some of these young students the thoroughness with which she knew them was scary! And her knowledge of them grew as they went on their various affiliations.

One of the unique things about the Nursing Department is that it was a community, as the Twelve chosen by Jesus were a community. And as the community of the Twelve centered around Jesus, so the community that was the Nursing Department centered around Sister Margaret Mary. And it was an ever growing community. You didn't leave it when you graduated. You continued to belong wherever you happened to be.

Sister Margaret Mary's concern followed her nurses wherever they went, somewhat in the same way that St. Paul managed to keep track of the churches he founded.

Indeed, the reading from the Epistle to the Philippians was chosen, because the Philippians were Paul's favorite group. Of all the churches, his heart went out to them the most. He kept in touch with them. He was concerned to know what was happening among them. And he found out – as he put it "either by seeing you myself or hearing about your behavior from a distance." And always his concern is to be sure that they stand firm in unity and in professing the faith of the Gospel. And that was Sister Margaret Mary too – seeing them herself or hearing about their behavior from a distance and praying they remain firm in unity and in the faith of the Gospel.

As I am sure you all know, St. Paul was not slow to lower the boom on any of his churches, if he felt they needed correction. And that applied to his beloved Philippians as well as the rest. I need not tell Nazareth College nurses that Sister Margaret Mary showed no more reluctance than Paul to correct and reprove when she felt it was needed.

I have to add, of course, that she reserved to herself the prerogative of being critical of the Nazareth College nurses. While she was never hesitant about exercising that prerogative, she made it quite clear that that prerogative was hers alone to exercise. Woebetide any of the rest of us who would dare assume the right to criticize her nurses.

Sister Margaret Mary was able to give herself in discipline, in love and concern to the nurses of Nazareth College, because she had already given herself fully to God. God had allured her, as Hosea puts it, had led her into the desert, spoken to her heart and espoused her to himself forever. She was devoted to her students because she was a good woman. But over and above that she was a religious and her commitment to the Nursing Department and its students was her ministry.

It is not that her nursing vocation and her religious commitment were two separate realities. Rather the one specified the other. She came to know her students in their uniqueness, but more than that she came to discover that the uniqueness of each of them was grounded in the God to Whom she had espoused herself. In finding them, she found Him also. In serving Him, she served them. Her religious commitment gave a unity to her life and to her ministry.

When she became a religious, she received the name Margaret. It is perhaps worth noting that her baptismal name was "Pearl" and that Margarita, the Latin form of her religious name, means "pearl." Jesus once told a story about a pearl-merchant who seeks a pearl of great worth and finally is able to claim it as his own.

We are here this morning, because God, the great Pearl-Merchant, has claimed Margaret Mary as His own. She who for so many months endured much suffering has entered at last into the joy of the Lord. The great Pearl-Merchant has taken to himself Margarita, the Pearl of Nazareth.

SR. IRENE WOLTER 6-24-2002

Readings: Is. 49:1-6
1Cor. 13: 4-13
Jn. 14:25-29

It is interesting to reflect that Sr. Irene's funeral is being celebrated on the feast of John the Baptist. The Baptist was a great saint, yet he lived in the background of larger events. He was not the bridegroom, but the friend of the bridegroom. He was not the Word, but only the voice. His glory was that Christ should increase and he should decrease. It doesn't take much imagination to see how appropriate to celebrate Sr. Irene's birthday into eternal life on the feast day of the birth of John the Baptist. She too lived in the background of larger events. In her 41 years at Nazareth College, she lived and acted largely behind the scenes. She did the things that nobody else wanted to do; yet they needed doing and she did them with love. What struck me immediately when I heard of her death was that she was a woman who did the many, many little things that are so important to make life smooth and enjoyable for others. And she did them with love.

One of the things, perhaps not so well known about her, is the quiet, gentle influence she had on students at Nazareth College during the 41 years she served there. She never taught in a classroom, but she was in touch with students on a more personal level. How many students we can't even guess. Here is one example: Saturday evening I was at a party and a woman whom I did not know told me about the daughter of a friend of hers who was a student at Nazareth and came under the influence of Sr. Irene. The young woman had a very poor image of herself and confided to Sr. Irene that she felt that she was unattractive and in so many ways not the equal of her classmates. She felt she didn't really fit in. Sr. Irene managed to get across to her that she was beautiful and attractive and that if she would just be herself people would like her. Apparently over time Sr. Irene was convincing. To this day that young woman is quick to say that her life was changed by her relationship with this dear sister who took the time to listen to the fears and insecurities of a young college student. She still remembers Sr. Irene with love and gratitude as the person who helped put her life together when it seemed to be falling apart.

There is a basic principle that should guide homilies or eulogies: "*Nil nisi optimum de mortuis*" which means "Say nothing but the best about the dead." In the case of Sr.

Irene this presents no problem. I can't think of anything to say about her but the best.

She was one of the few persons about whom it can honestly be said: you simply cannot praise her enough. Everybody loved her. There was a sturdy gentleness about her. She would do anything for people, yet she was no doormat for anyone. In her quiet way she expected respect for her work and her person. All the adjectives that Paul pours out in 1st Corinthians in speaking about love were realized in her: patient, kind, not envious or boastful or arrogant, not irritable or resentful, rejoicing in the truth. If there were flaws in her character, I suspect all of us would be hard pressed to find a single one. She was, as I say, one of the few persons whom you can only praise.

On Friday, the feast of St. Aloysius Gonzaga, Sr. Irene drew her last breath. We know that recently she had great difficulty in breathing. Breathing is one of the great mysteries of life that we take for granted, till we see someone whose breathing is difficult and labored. Breathing and living are closely connected. Before medical science developed more sophisticated ways of determining death, the oldest way of knowing that a person was dead was to hold a mirror to the person's mouth. If the mirror remained unblurred, that showed that the person was no longer breathing and consequently it meant that the person was dead.

This is a physiological way of viewing death: it means the cessation of breathing. But our faith assures us that the ceasing of breathing which marks the end of one's earthly life, is, in a theological sense, a passover to a new life, where there is a wholly different kind of breathing. For a Christian death is learning to breath in a new way: with the free and unlabored breath of the Holy Spirit.

The Greek word used in the New Testament for the Holy Spirit is the word ***pneuma***. It is a word rich in meaning. At the created level its primary meaning is "wind" or "breath" or "spirit." Most often when it is used in the New Testament it refers to God, to our participation in God's life, in God's "breathing," in God's Spirit. When we speak of God's Holy Spirit, we could just as easily speak of God's Holy Breath.

Before Friday last, ***pneuma*** often meant for Sr. Irene that difficult, labored breathing that she had to put up with. But now the word ***pneuma*** takes on the highest possible meaning. Because she has been taken into God, it is God's Breath, God's Spirit, who breathes in her now. United as she now is to God, it is God's Breath that breathes in her now. Listen to the Gospel and hear the promise Christ made that his return to God would mean that God would send the divine Spirit, the holy Breath on us. What will one day happen to all of us – the full receiving of the Holy Spirit, the Holy Breath, has already happened to Sr. Irene.

The beautiful hymn we are using in today's liturgy fits this occasion so perfectly:

> O breathe on me, Thou Breath of God.
> Fill me with life anew.

The last verse is right on:

> O breath on me, Thou Breath of God,
> So shall I never die,
> But live with you the perfect life of your eternity.

Dear Sister Irene, you no longer need an artificial respirator to enable you to breathe easily. For you are linked to the divine Respirator, the Holy Giver of Breath. The Holy Spirit, the Holy Breath dwells in you in the fullness of the divine Presence. Breathe deeply with freedom and in the joy and peace of your heavenly home.

SR. MARIE MARTIN MADIGAN   7-20-2002

Readings: Micah 6:6-8
2 Tim 4: 6-8
Mt. 25: 31-40

It's very hard to talk about a dear friend and try to
say what it meant have her as a friend – this wonderful lady
with the winsome smile that lighted up her face. One thing
I am very happy to be able to say: not many days before her
stroke we had lunch – at a superb restaurant – where in just
a couple of hours we solved all the problems of Church and
country. The last bit of writing I gave her was "An Open
Letter to the American Bishops" in which I took the

bishops to task for a number of ways in which I felt they were failing to lead priests and laity in the Church as they should. She enjoyed reading it and is now in a position to address those concerns to Higher Authority. I am glad too that a few days before her stroke I sent her a copy of **Paradise Journey**. In a letter she sent after getting the book she said more than she perhaps realized at the time: she spoke of her own personal "nostalgia for paradise" and her readiness to take that "paradise journey." Now we know that, in the words of the poet, she has "rubbed death out of her eyes" and completed that perilous but glorious journey into God, into divine Goodness and Beauty.

She was a highly gifted woman with many talents. Perhaps her giftedness could be summed up in a few words that Sr. Maria Elena said to me a few days ago: "She created beauty wherever she went." Beauty is something that is easily misunderstood in our technological, utilitarian world. True beauty is goodness that shines with luster. True beauty is something that cannot be described; it can only be experienced. It is an experience beyond words that touches profound recesses of our being and awakens us to a world beyond life's daily grind. Today, I venture to say, this chapel is filled with people who in wonderful and highly varied ways have experienced the beauty that emanated from our dear sister, Marie Martin –a beauty that changed their lives.

She was beauty in action: whether in making a beautiful bouquet for a birthday or for someone who was sick; or a delicious meal, and the meal might be intended to feed her friends or to feed the hungry. Both were done with the same loving care. She knew that the poor had as great a claim on her love as her friends. Maybe perhaps even greater.

She was beauty in action when she opening the minds and hearts of children to the talents hidden inside them:, talents that were yearning to burst forth; and it was Marie Martin's loving touch that brought them forth. I wonder how many people are here today whose childhood years were enriched by that loving touch. It was the touch of beauty. She saw beauty not only in the face of a child, but also in the face of the elderly person. The aged are not just "specimens" of aging humanity. They are wondrous temples of God, persons of unutterable beauty. They have traveled to the threshold of eternity and are waiting to be called into the beauty of their God.

Sr. Marie Martin was beauty in action when she spoke about the Church she loved. It was a love that was not blind or thoughtless. She was in the vanguard of all the movements in the Church that looked for needed reform. She saw those reforms as a call to action. Indeed, her love for the Church was a tough love: she loved the Church, not so much for what it is but for what with God's grace it is able to become.

Her charm, her grace, her beauty were not just on the surface, not only did they reach and open up something deep in so many of us, they expressed something deep inside her: the spark of divinity in her that shone forth in what she said and did. It was God's love manifested in her person: her love for God, for people and for all God's good creation. It was a love that especially and instinctively reached out to all who needed her. Peace and justice were not just words for her. They were goals she gave her life to in whatever way she could. She heard and took very seriously –not simply as something to meditate on but as call to action, a call to serve people --the words of the prophet Micah: Here is what the Lord requires of you: "to do justice and to love kindness and to walk humbly with your God." Marie Martin in her concern for people would surely have identified with the words of the poet, Edna St. Vincent Millay: "O world, I cannot hold thee close enough."

How wonderfully she embodied in her life the spirit of the Gospel we have just heard: this Gospel of mistaken identity, this Gospel that tells us that we find Jesus and experience his presence in the needy stranger. Marie Martin knew that. She lived it.

Whether she would describe it in this way or not, her view of life and reality was sacramental and incarnational. She saw Christ in others. They were the signs of his presence for her. Whether she was always conscious of it or not, her life story shows that she saw beyond life's surface to a transcendent dimension of reality. Her life and understanding contrasted with many of us who so seldom plumb the depths of reality. Like Elizabeth Barrett Browning she saw that "Earth's crammed with heaven And every common bush afire with God." Or, like Gerard Manley Hopkins she caught glimpses of a "world charged with the grandeur of God."

For those who love beauty in this life, there is a way of understanding that death too, in an altogether unique way, is beauty in action. I am not referring to dying which is almost always painful and unpleasant. It is not easy to die. We have to wait till it happens. There is a passivity about dying: it is passive in the sense that it happens to us. It is beyond our control.

But death is something very different. It is something we do. It is an action. At the moment of death, in a way that bystanders cannot see, a person stands before God, stands face to face with divine Goodness, divine Beauty and says "Yes" to God. Death is a moment of absolute clarity and complete freedom. All the things that might distract us in this life are gone. All through life we say a "Yes" to God that is sometimes firm, sometimes hesitant. At death there is no longer anything to prevent us from speaking out a resounding and joyful "Yes" to God.

If throughout her life Marie Martin was beauty in action, even more so her death was "beauty in action." In that moment of death's "tremendous nearness" she experienced, not just something beautiful, but Beauty Itself. For Beauty is the name of God.

SR. JEANNE TROY 12-17-1994

Readings: Isaiah 35: 1-10
John 14: 1-6

"Come, Lord Jesus, come!" "Into your hands, O Lord, I commend my spirit!" For days these words rang out in Sr. Jeanne's room. They were said by Jeanne, as long as she was able; and then when she could no longer speak, they were said by her friends on her behalf. Yes, during the past week the third floor of the Motherhouse resounded with the words of these two prayers: "Come, Lord Jesus, come," and "Into your hands, O Lord, I commend my spirit."

"Come, Lord Jesus" is an advent cry. It is a cry to the Lord Jesus who is always present with us to come with the absolute fullness of his presence. It is a cry that springs from the lips of all of us, each year during the advent season. And each year it happens and it doesn't happen. Each year, the Lord Jesus enters ever more deeply into our lives; but each year, we have to make the humble admission: "It really hasn't happened yet. Jesus has not yet come with the absolute fullness of his presence."

But what is true of all of us assembled here is no longer true of Sr. Jeanne. Like all of us, she spent many advents waiting for that total coming of her Saviour. But it didn't happen. It didn't happen, that is, till this year, 1994. Advent of 1994, she cried out: "Come, Lord Jesus, come." Jesus came and answered her call. He came in the fullness of his presence. He came to fulfill his promise: "I will come and I will take you to myself, so that where I am you also may be."

Have you ever stood on a wintry street corner waiting for a friend to come? You wait and wait. Finally the friend turns up. Your inclination is to say: "What took you so long?" I wonder if those might not have been Jeanne's first words at 6:06 a.m. Thursday morning when at long last the Lord Jesus came to claim his bride and take her to himself. I wonder if she didn't say, in that soft yet determined tone of voice she had: "I have been waiting a long time. Where have you been? What took you so long to come to me?"

Or maybe she didn't ask that question. Maybe she knew the answer. For, remember, there was that other prayer: "Into your hands, O Lord, I commend my spirit." This is not an advent prayer. It is a "passion prayer." It is Jesus' prayer from the cross. It is his prayer in the midst of his suffering. It is his prayer of total resignation to God and to God's will. "Spirit" means "breath." What Jesus is saying to God is: Every breath I have drawn in life has been for you. Now I hand over to you my breath, my last breath, all I have left. I hand all over to you."

That was what Jeanne was saying to God, as she lay seemingly helpless in her room on the third floor: "I have given my life to you. Now I want to give you my death. I want to give you my last breath." And, as her friends watched her breathing and no longer able to speak, they knew she was saying those words: "Into your hands, O Lord, I commend my sprit, my breath." And it was a sign of the completeness with which she gave her life, that she kept breathing and breathing, until finally she came to her last breath and God accepted it. We say, "she expired." That is not a euphemism for saying she died. It is rather a description of what death is. It means she gave up her spirit, her breath. She gave it back to God from whom it came.

If you look at the Gospel story of Jesus' passion, you will find that the three synoptic Gospels, when they describe Jesus' death, simply say: "He expired. He took his last breath." The Fourth Gospel, however, puts it differently. It says that Jesus "handed over his spirit." Scripture scholars see this as a Pentecostal event. In the very act of dying Jesus not only handed over his spirit to God. He also handed over His spirit, the Holy Spirit, to those whom he loved. Through his Spirit, Jesus continues to live on in his disciples.

Some people, when they die, simply expire. They return to God who made them and are filled with eternal joy. But there are some few people who, somewhat like Jesus, do more than expire; they hand over something of their spirit and live on in those whom they loved in life. For such people, death means more than just expiring, more than simply breathing their last. The influences they have had on people's lives, the way they have spent their energies, often against great odds, for the benefit of God's people and especially for God's poor and neglected and handicapped – all these create a spirit that such persons leave behind them. As it were, somewhat like Jesus, they hand over their spirit and that spirit continues, even after death, to influence the lives of many people.

Sr. Jeanne had a spirit that nothing seemed to daunt. Obstacles to her were not stumbling blocks, but challenges she was determined to meet – and meet head on. Indeed, the obstacles she had to face seemed to spur her on with great strength and determination. There are many people here today, and many who would be here if they could, who will continue to be influenced by her. Something of her spirit has been handed over to them. And their lives will be changed for the better because of that spirit.

In the Hebrew Scriptures, that which keeps people alive is the breath of God in them. When people die their breath returns to God. Thursday Jeanne died into God. That breath of God in her returned to its source. She has achieved full awareness of her oneness with God. She is fully in God and God is fully in her. And all this is sheer joy, boundless happiness, and pure delight. It is hers forever more. And we can only thank God. The One who is mighty has done great things for her.

I want to offer a word of comfort to Mother Agnes Cecilia to Jeanne's friends at Lourdes, to her colleagues at Nazareth -- especially those in the music department and to all the friends who were so often with her and loved her. The Christian life is one of letting go. It is hard to imagine a greater "letting go" than Mother Agnes Cecilia's letting go of one to whom she was both sister and "mother." Yet she has given her up with that courage and Christian commitment that has always marked her life.

Jeanne realized how difficult this would be for Agnes Cecilia. Before she lost consciousness, Jeanne said to me: "There is something I want you to do for me." "What is it?" I asked her. "I want you to take care of my sister." I figured I could say yes to that with an easy heart and with a sense that there wouldn't be much I would have to do. These Troy ladies are strong people, quite able to take care of themselves. In fact, I'm quite convinced that if the Troys of Rochester had been present at the legendary Troy of ancient times, the Greeks would never have won the Trojan War and Homer would never have written the Iliad.

And thus, my friends, we come together today because Jeanne's odyssey is over. She who dwelt in the shadows of darkness dwells now in unapproachable light. We come not so much to pray for her, as to remember her. We come to share the wisdom she learned, the bravery she lived. We come to catch some of the spirit she has handed over to us.

Good by, sweet sister,
May flights of angels sing thee to thy rest.

SR. THERESE LANG 5-31-1995

Readings: Hosea 2: 14-15
Philippians 3: 7-14
John 16: 10-17

During the last several weeks I felt the need to go visit Sr. Therese at the Infirmary. It was not so much that she needed me to come as that I needed to go. I can only express the feeling of going into her room as a feeling of awe. Being with her in these last days was truly an awesome experience. I know the world "awesome" has been trivialized to mean almost anything special. But I use the word "awe" in its most literal meaning: that sense of reverence, wonder, amazement that is experienced when one knows that he or she is in the presence of God. Yet awe is more than just experiencing that God is there; it is experiencing that God is doing things right before your eyes. You experience not only that God is in a place, but that God is doing things there.

What was God doing in her Infirmary room? God was transforming Therese. What was going on in her before our very eyes? She was undergoing a conversion experience. But a special conversion experience: that final conversion in which one comes to realize that God is all and that, in ultimate terms, nothing else matters. But the awesome part of this conversion is that once one sees that nothing save God truly matters, you begin to see that everything matters, but only in God. It is a whole new vision of reality, a wonderful, awesome experience of enlightenment.

The Christian life for all of us is a series of conversions, as more and more we yield to God's actions in our lives, as more and more we surrender to the divine blandishments. I had almost said that in our final conversion we yield to the divine seduction. I do not hesitate to use the word "seduction," because the Hebrew word used in our first reading comes very close to saying that. "I will allure her and bring her into the desert." It is as if the sacred writer is saying God uses all the divine wiles to bring her into the closest intimacy with the Divine Self.

The desert, in the terminology of Christian spirituality, means two things. It is a place of temptation. It is a place of divine intimacy. The desert experience of Therese's last illness meant temptation: the temptation to deny it, to say: "No, this is not happening to me. This is not what God is asking of me."

But her desert experience in the past few weeks took on that other meaning which the desert has signified in Christian spirituality: it became the experience of divine intimacy. It is no exaggeration to say that going into her room at the Infirmary one felt the presence of grace. As her voice grew weaker, she was content to say: "God has been so good to me. God has been so good to me." She could also have said those moving words from Philippians: "Jesus Christ has made me his own." For in truth that is what had happened.

The divine wiles were at work in her and she surrendered to God's allurement, to the magnetism of the divine presence, as the Lord Jesus made her his own. And all at once the desert into which she had been lured flowered. There was no longer bareness, emptiness. There was beauty and loveliness far beyond the beauty of lilacs, dogwood and tulips. There was the beauty of paradise.

Yes, in her last illness Therese acquired a marvelous simplicity. At the heart of that simplicity was a divine intimacy that is hidden in all of us, but which so many of us do not experience till after death. St. Augustine expressed that intimacy in striking terms. In his prayer to God in the third book of the Confessions, he says to God: "Tu eras interior intimo meo." A sentence impossible to translate. An approximation would be: "You were inside my most intimate reality." Or one could put it this way: "When I find my own deepest reality, I find that you are there."

If the first reading suggests, as one way of expressing that intimacy with God, the divine espousals whereby Christ Jesus had made her his own, the Gospel describes that intimacy in terms of deep friendship. Jesus speaks of the Christian conversion (and this would apply to all the conversions we experience through life, but especially apply to the final conversion experience) in terms of a transition from being servants to being friends. The close and loving friendship that Therese shared with Sr. Mary Wehner and her warm relationship with her brother and his family were, as it were, paradigms of the indescribable intimacy with God that is involved in being brought into the inner circle of God's friends. Jesus tells us the difference between being God's servant (an important role indeed) and being God's friend. A servant is not privy to her Master's counsels; a friend is.

All through life God leads us; but the ambiguities of life are very much present. Clarity of vision comes at the end for those who have the privilege of going through a dying process such as Sr. Therese experienced.

As she neared the end, she knew that God alone matters, that God sufficed. She knew this, for she was already experiencing the mystery of Jesus' death and resurrection. Like Paul, she wanted only to "know Christ and the power of his resurrection and the sharing of his suffering by becoming like him in his death." She could say with Paul: "For the sake of Christ I have suffered the loss of all things. Indeed I regard them as rubbish compared to attaining Christ and sharing in the power of his resurrection... All I want to do is to press on to the goal: the heavenly call of God in Christ Jesus."

What does Paul mean when he speaks of suffering the loss of all things and indeed regarding them as rubbish? Does this mean that Therese should look back at her work in building the Chemistry Department at Nazareth College, in participating in the Science Morality Conferences, in the research she did at the Max Planck Institute, in teaching her students, in the loving contacts she had with her brother and family over the years and her relationships with her colleagues and all her friends – does this mean that she should look upon all these as so much rubbish? By no means. God's wonderful creation and all that it entails is rubbish only if we see it as apart from God and from the divine love that brought all these things into being. They are "rubbish" only when they turn us away from God.

If you don't like the word "rubbish" to describe our stance toward the world (and I admit my own ambivalence about the word Paul uses), you might prefer the milder term of Thomas Aquinas. After a deep experience of God, he said: "Compared to what I have experienced, all else is but straw."

Indeed, you might prefer, as even better, Julian of Norwich and her gentler way. She describes the world as a HAZEL NUT.

God showed me a little thing, the size of a hazel nut and He told me that this is everything that is. And I marveled that it could exist because it was so small. Then I realized that it exists, because God loves it.

What I am wanting to suggest is that to experience the power of the resurrection is not to deny the wonderfulness of all the human realities and relationships that make up our lives. It is to appreciate them all the more. It is to have them placed in a new context, in which they mean not less to us, but more. For the more we experience the power of Christ's resurrection, the stronger our relationships become. For we see them where they have always been: namely, in God who is ALL, and they are no longer weakened by any kind selfishness or self-seeking. But still, compared to the greatness of God, they are tiny like the hazel nut, yet wonderful because loved by God.

On another occasion God spoke to Julian in those well known words: "All shall be well. You shall see that every manner of things shall be well."

Thus, Julian said: "God showed me that He cares not only for great and noble things, but equally for small and little and lowly things. This is what he meant when he told me: 'Everything shall be all right.'"

This was Julian's simple way of expressing the hidden dynamism of the mystery of the resurrection working in the lives of God's lovers and friends. We live in God and God lives in us. But not only we but all those who are dear to us and, indeed,, all of reality.

"All shall be well." For us this is an eschatological reality we shall experience at the end. For Sr. Therese, it is a present experience. She knows now: "Everything is well." She would say to Mary Wehner and to her family and to all her friends and to all of us: "Yes, everything is well. Take courage. Everything is all right and good and wonderful." And for this we praise God and offer Eucharist which means Thanksgiving!

*****

The readings for this liturgy (Hosea 2: 14-15; Philippians 3: 7-14; John 16: 10-17) are the same readings Sr. Therese chose for her silver jubilee which she celebrated on June 25, 1982.

SR. GRACE GEISLER 1-10-1997

Readings: 1 John 2: 29; 3:1-3
Luke 2: 16-21

At the midnight Mass on Christmas, Pope John Paul II spoke of joy in the birth of God who becomes one of us. He went on to say: "The Son of God does not come into the world empty-handed. It is true that in the stable of Bethlehem, He receives the gifts of the shepherds, but first He Himself brings great gifts...Precisely that great gift which the Apostle Paul called 'grace.'"

Tonight I would like to say that God has given a gift to the Sisters of St. Joseph for 64 years and to Nazareth College for many of those years, a great gift which we call "Grace" – Sr. Grace Geisler. She has been a "grace" to so many of us. In her gentle, quiet way she has in her own life helped us to see what it means to be children of God. For as the Epistle of John says: "That is really what we are: children of God. But so often we don't realize it."

Someone spoke to me about Sr. Grace, when she was at the college: "Grace will never get an ulcer," this person said, "She is too easy-going." She had a great mind, was a "cracker-jack teacher, kindly yet insistent." But she carried her knowledge humbly and without show. She was indeed unflappable, relaxed and without "spot or wrinkle." I sent an E-Mail message to a former teacher in the Biology department, Doris Zallen who now lives in Blacksburg, Virginia. I got her return e-mail this morning. She said: "Her name really suited her... I will keep trying to emulate her calm and her good humor."

Sr. Grace took life in stride. There was a blessed ordinariness about her. She knew the gifts she had from God (and they were abundant). She used them unto God's praise and for the good of her students and of her beloved family. I don't think there was an envious bone in her body. She rejoiced in the gifts God had given to others, just as much as she rejoiced in her own gifts.

She did not live her life or use her gifts by comparison. I doubt she ever thought she would want to be someone else or have someone else's gifts. She was quite content just to be herself. For so many of us that is not an easy thing to do. All too easily we compare our gifts with those of others and wonder if we ourselves may be found wanting. So many people are unhappy because they want to be somebody else. We feel so often the need to be affirmed, to receive the approval of others. Affirmation and approval by others is often the condition of our own happiness. Over and over again we feel the need of "proving" ourselves.

That was not a problem for Grace. It was enough for her to be what she could be and to do what she could do. Her refusal to live her life by comparison can be the great grace that she offers us: the grace to enjoy being ourselves, the grace to enjoy whatever gifts God has given to us, and to be satisfied and happy with that.

In her last years Sr. Grace was more retiring. She seemed to be more alone. Like Mary at Bethlehem, she pondered and treasured in her heart all that God had done for her. She often walked alone, as if she were on a journey. And in a sense she was. She had, I think, that strange unanalyzable sense that some people have, especially toward the end of their lives, of stronger and stronger bonds that link us with another world that is our true home and that we have to get to. There was the vision of another world that was becoming more and more real to her. Zosima the Elder in Dostoevsky's novel, *The Brothers Karamazov,* speaks of the bonds we have with this other world:

Much on earth is concealed from us, but in place of it we have been granted a secret, mysterious sense of our living bonds with the other world, with the higher heavenly world;…the roots of our thoughts and feelings are not here but in that other world.

He speaks of the seeds God sows in us that are from that other world and can only sprout and come to full bloom in the world from which they came. In other words, we have to go to that other world to be fully ourselves. It is only there that we are truly at home.

Yet when we distinguish this world and that other world, we must be careful not to think that we are talking about geography. That other world does not exist apart from this world, say like another planet might exist in our solar system apart from planet earth. No, that other world commingles with this world. We can discover it, if only partially, in this life.

Death is the full discovery of that other world – that was always there, but we didn't know it. For that other world is the life of God communicated to us: partially in this life, fully in death. Death is finding a place to dwell in that is truly home. We have here no lasting city. We are looking for the city that is to come. Yet the paradox is that we are already in it. But we have to discover that we are there. Our prayer, our deeds, our loves, our joys and sorrows are all ways in which we make that discovery. Death is the final step in that discovery. Death is not going some where. It's finding Someone. For we die into God. We dwell in God and God dwells in us. We return to God who is our home.

Can't you picture Sr. Grace's family and friends, who have already passed through the portal of death to that other world greeting her on last Tuesday and rejoicing with her?

Sr. Grace loved her family and there were quite a lot of them to love. She never forgot an anniversary, a birthday, and an illness that needed prayers. So many times she would leave notes for me in the chapel vestry asking me to pray for father, mother, brother, sister, nephew, niece – on just such occasions.

Toward the end, the pull of that other world became so great that she simply stopped eating. It is almost as if she forgot to eat. Her thoughts were elsewhere. Today when the issue of "assisted suicide" is before the Supreme Court and being widely discussed, we need to realize the huge difference between wanting to be helped to take one's life and the longing to be with God. There was not in Sr. Grace even the breath of a death wish. But all her life, especially the end, was dominated by a God-wish: the desire to be with God, the joy of achieving the goal of her journey, the joy of being fully with God.

SR. STELLA REGINA WELCH 11-23-1993

Readings: 1 Corinthians 15: 35-41
John 17: 24-26

I was fascinated Sunday to read in the *New York Times* the interview with Lewis Thomas. As you know, he is a physician and a biologist who achieved fame by writing about biology in a way that interested people who were not biologists. No small feat indeed. That a book with a title, *The Lives of the Cell* would become a best-seller was truly a literary phenomenon.

But the *Times* interview was not about biology; it was about dying and about Lewis Thomas's reflections on death. It is a moving article, deeply spiritual in its own way, but devoid of any explicit religious content. He sees love as the indispensable reality of life, but knows of no Source from which love derives. He sees a universe carefully planned, but no Planner. He seems to believe in the soul, but not one that is immortal.

I was impressed with this article. Lewis Thomas is what I would call an exemplary secular humanist. By that I mean a person who has a deep sense of fundamental human, spiritual and cosmic values, but no sense of God, no sense of a life with God after this life. Or, to put it in a different way (and I don't mean this to sound arrogant), he has a sense of God, but doesn't know it. He doesn't know it, because he cannot articulate it. And one of the things that get in his way is the very wrong impressions of what the word God means that he received from whatever religious source he may have been in contact with. He gives this away when he says at one point that if you believed in God and in immortality, you would have to dress death up with the notions of rewards and penalties. "I don't think that's reasonable," he says.

I don't think it's reasonable, either, to "dress death up with notions of rewards and penalties." I see death as something very different: something Lewis Thomas never thought of --at least explicitly. Death, I see, as the great Door of entry into the very reality of God. But that entry into God is not a reward but a fulfillment A fulfillment of all the things Lewis Thomas believed in. But, sadly, he does not seem to believe in such a fulfillment. I am sorry he doesn't believe in it. What I am confident of is that God believes in him.

We gather here tonight because we do believe in death as a fulfillment. In a sense, everything that happens to us in life pales into insignificance when compared to what happens to us in death. Someone once defined life in this way: "Life is what you do while you are waiting for death." And there is a lot to be said for the validity of such a statement. It doesn't mean that what you do in life is unimportant. But everything we do -- growing up, getting a job, embracing a vocation, getting married, having children, getting degrees, writing books --all these may represent certain peak moments in life. But none of them can rival that climactic moment: that moment we call death, that moment in which we say a full and total "Yes" to God and are wrapped around by the arms of a loving God.

Death is not the end of a contest, where prizes or penalties are handed out to winners and losers. Death is going home, to the only home that can satisfy our deepest longings and desires. Death is the open door to total happiness. I hope that when he does die Lewis Thomas will experience this. I am confident that he will.

We come here tonight to celebrate Sr. Stella Regina's death with a sense of joy and hope and consolation. There is surely a deep sense of loss for all the many people who loved her. But we must take joy and peace from the realization that this experience is not loss, but rather all gain, for Stella.

Sr. Stella Regina was something of a paradox. She was, in many ways, a very private person. There are not, I would venture, many people with whom she shared her deepest thoughts and deepest moments of faith. But there is the curious fact, the paradox that, though there were not many whom she let into her own inner life, there are hundreds and hundreds in many, many places whose lives she entered into, often deeply and intimately, and who loved her, because they knew she cared.

She was a most beloved dean of freshmen. In fact she rewrote the book on what it means to be dean of freshmen. When women and men came to Nazareth for their first year, it wasn't long before they knew Sr. Stella. It wasn't long either till she knew them and all about them. They learned very quickly that there just wasn't any kind of wool around that they could pull over her eyes. She knew when they were good and when they were bad. In either case she knew what to do and what she had to say to them. And she was never slow in saying it. If one of them disappeared, it was Sr. Stella who found them. If they were failing courses, she was after them to improve. If they were doing well, she was always there to encourage them. If they had problems (and I'm still close enough to academic life to know that freshmen always have problems), she was available to counsel them and to advise them and to console them.

Nor did she lose sight of them when they ceased to be freshmen. The bonds made in that freshman year were too strong to be broken simply by passage out of the freshman class. That is why, if the truth were known she was advisor to half the student body, whatever their class might be. And that is why when the alumnae returned to the College for reunion, Sr. Stella was one of the people they most frequently asked to see. For they loved her. And they loved her because they knew that she cared.

Last night, after the prayer service, I met a most lovely young woman, Cheryl Bell. She told me she was graduated from Nazareth last year. "Sr. Stella," told me, was with me for four years. Nazareth won't be Nazareth for me without Sr. Stella.

Some of us who go back a number of decades of Nazareth College history remember the unforgettable and inimitable Rosemary White. We also remember that heaven was much on her mind, because she talked so often of the school she was going to have in heaven. I don't know whether or not there is a school in heaven; but if there is, I am sure that Stella has already put in her application for the position of dean of freshmen. And with the extraordinary resume she has, she is a shoo-in for the position.

Stella, new star in the heavenly firmament, we pray for you tonight. Not because we believe that you need our prayers. For we are confident that God has enfolded you in the divine love that is inexpressible joy. But we pray, because our prayers are a way that a loving God has given us to keep our contacts with those whom God has called to the Divine Presence. Our prayers are our way of embracing you, our way of experiencing the communion of saints. Because of the communion of saints, we know that we are one with you in God.

SR. XAVIER DONEGAN 12-28-1994

Readings: Titus 3: 4-7
Luke 2: 15-20

On Christmas morning at 9:00 a.m., just before we began our Christmas liturgy here at the Motherhouse, Sr. Xavier slipped quietly into heaven. I choose those words with care. For that is exactly as we might imagine her doing it: slipping quietly, unobtrusively, inconspicuously into heaven. She would not have wanted any fuss made over her coming. In a self-effacing way she would just have wanted to blend into the picture, take her place there, and do whatever one is supposed to do in heaven.

Some people live their lives on the outside. They are content with the superficial. They hardly ever touch the deepest recesses of their own being. As a result, they go through life not really knowing who they are, except at a very superficial level of being.

There are other people who live their lives on the inside. What matters most to them is hidden. It seems to me that Sr. Xavier was such a person, living more on the inside than on the outside. Like Mary, she treasured the gifts of God and pondered them in her heart. Her heart was the place of rendezvous with the Inward Stranger. She could relish the divine Mystery within her and reflect on it. Perhaps in words like Merton's:

> Closer and clearer
> Than any wordy master,
> Thou inward Stranger
> Whom I have never seen.
> Deep and cleaner
> Than the clamorous ocean
> Seize up my silence
> Hold me in thy Hand.

The twinkle in her eyes and the smile on her face perhaps concealed more than it revealed.

She was, in many ways, a very private person. There are not, I would venture, many people with whom she shared her deepest thoughts and most profound moments of faith. The paradox of her life was that she tended to be withdrawn, yet her love and concern for people and her desire to help them were obvious and prominent characteristics of her life and ministry. She was one who gave rather than one who took. The paradox was that she served many, yet was close to few. It may be that the resolution of the paradox is this: prizing, as she did, the hiddenness of her own life, she hesitated to intrude into the deeper recesses of the lives of others. She put a high value on her own inner being and therefore respected the inviolable inner reality of others. Perhaps in another age she might have been a Julian of Norwich, living in quietness and solitude, yet ministering constantly to those who sought her help.

Comparing her to Julian of Norwich is not as far fetched as it might seem. The day after her death, Sr. Anna Louise told me that Xavier's favorite song, one she loved to sing with the beautiful voice she had, was the song "In a Monastery Garden." I thought of singing this song at this point in my homily. But the chair of the Music Department at Nazareth College absolutely forbade me to do so. You will never know what you missed.

It is surely significant that she who valued quiet so profoundly died on Christmas day: the day that Christ the Saviour slipped silently and unobtrusively into our world, the day that is at last a day of quiet and relaxation for people whose lives have been taken up with a great deal of busyness in the days preceding.

The people who come into our lives in a significant way are like angelic beings: they come to us with a message from God. What is the word that God would teach us through Sr. Xavier?

Perhaps the word spoken to us in Sr. Xavier is a call to realize how much our lives are taken up with what doesn't really matter. The word God speaks to us through her is a call to find the depths of our own spirits that the trivialities and illusions of everyday existence often hide from us.

The goal of human life is to become more real. To become fully real is to enter into God. Deep down in the hearts of all of us is a spark of diversity known only to God and inaccessible to all others. In a sense, life is a search to find that spark and in the finding of it to come to realize our oneness with God.

I spoke earlier about Xavier slipping into heaven. Yet heaven is not really a place that we go to. Heaven is a discovery of that inner place, that is really no place at all, where we are one with God and in God one with all that is. We have to get over our notion of heaven as a kind of Hawaiian Intercontinental hotel, which is first empty and then begins to fill up as guests arrive who have the proper reservations. In reality, heaven isn't a place we go to. It is becoming ourselves fully and totally. And we find that fullness of being only in God.

Sr. Xavier has achieved that fullness and the overwhelming joy that it brings. We are pilgrims on the way toward that fullness of joy. Through Sr. Xavier God calls us not just to travel forward, but to travel inward, as it were, to travel into the depths of our own being, where alone we find God and our own true selves. That Monastery Garden she used to sing about was not a physical place; it was the garden in the hidden abyss of her own heart.

SR. THERESA DANIEL KNAPP 2-11-2003

Readings: Rev. 21:1-5
1 Jn, 4: 7-12
Jn. 14:1-3

I know you are a staunch Republican, Theresa. I hope you're not upset that a Democrat is giving your homily!

We are all adjusting to a new situation: a new home. Remember over the past year or more how much we talked about the *new* Motherhouse, wondering if it would ever be finished and if we would ever make it there? Now "there" has become "here." We have brought our boxes and emptied them. We have accepted the invitation to enter into a new building and upon a new life style. We are happy with the new Motherhouse, though we don't quite know what to call the other one. It seems like an act of disloyalty not to call it the Motherhouse, but as we grow accustomed to this building and enjoy its beauty– the chapel, our rooms, the hallways, the memories that flood us as we turn a corner and see a beautiful painting or a statue that we love – we experience a sense of happiness and gratitude that we are here indeed and that we belong here. We are ready now to call this *the* Motherhouse.

The joy we had in coming here was something that Sr. Theresa Daniel wanted to share with us and we are all so happy that she was able to come to die in this new building that has become our home. Of all who came to this building she is the one person who came here to die. She wanted to experience this new motherhouse. But she knew that this would not be her home for long. She knew that another –far better – home was being readied for her; and, as her strength grew weaker, her desire to go to that new and more wondrous home became stronger. That desire was fulfilled on Sunday morning when she died in the arms of her ever-faithful nurse, Donna Warner. Donna, who was with her through the night, told me that just at the moment she took her last breath, she lifted her head, looked up, as if to say: "I'm coming. I'm coming home. I am coming to my new home." I am reminded of St. Stephen, the first martyr, who at the moment of his death looked up to heaven and said: "I see the heavens opened and the Son of Man standing at the right hand of God."

There is an immense difference between our coming here to a new home and Theresa going home to God. We come not only with our boxes; we come also as the persons we are with the qualities we have developed over our lifetime. We come with our virtues – and there are so many wonderful virtues in this community -- but also --I am sure we would all be ready to admit --- we come with the faults and failings that we all are ready to acknowledge.

Let me put it this way: the circumstances of our lives have been transformed, but not the persons we are. All our baggage – material and spiritual, good or bad -- we have brought with us to this new building. If our lives are to be transformed, this will be accomplished not by coming to a new building, but by deepening our desire to say "Yes" to God in all aspects of our lives. Saying Yes to God is something we are good at sometimes and not so good at other times. But we keep trying.

Sunday morning Theresa said "Yes" to God with a fullness and depth that we –trying as we will – simply cannot achieve in this life. She spoke a "Yes" to God that she had never before been able to say with the absolute fullness of spirit as she did on the moment when she breathed her last, and in that moment looked up and saw the face of God. All that remained of human weakness in her melted away in the warmth of that holy vision. Theresa had been transformed by divine Love. She had entered into that circulation of love that is the life of the Holy Trinity. Last week, on one occasion when I visited her, we talked about the love of God, and our belief that God is love. I suggested to her that, when we think of God's love, we need to be aware of its uniqueness. The very essence of God's love is to circulate. By that I mean, God's love goes from one divine Self to another without ever finding a Self that blocks or impedes that flow of love. The blessed in heaven are taken into that circulation of love and in it they find their total fulfillment.

In Monday's Office there was a reading from St. Bonaventure that describes the life of the blessed in heaven in these beautiful words:

When we do live that life, we shall understand fully, we shall love completely, and our desires will be totally satisfied. Then, with all our needs fulfilled, we shall truly know the love that surpasses understanding and so be filled with the fullness of God. (Breviary, Reading, Monday, week 4)

When people come to this Motherhouse for a wake or a funeral, they are sometimes surprised to find that the overriding emotion they experience here is not sadness (though that certainly is present). The overriding emotion is joy. We rejoice in a life fulfilled. So today we have to rejoice that Theresa is now filled with the fullness of God.

Whatever may be the attitude elsewhere, in this house we have a very distinctive understanding of death. We know, for instance, that death is different from dying. Dying is a process over which we have no control. But death is very different from dying. For death is not a *passion*, that is something that happens to us. Rather death is an *action*. It is something we do. Death is the moment of total freedom. Nothing in us impedes us from entering into the fullness of God. It is the moment of total transformation, when we come to understand what the Risen Jesus meant when he said: "I make all things new." (Rev. 21:5)

R. S. Thomas, the Welsh poet, speaks of death as being overwhelmed by the reality of God.

> As I had always known
> He would come, unannounced...
> I looked at him, not with the eye
> Only, but with the whole
> of my being, overflowing with
> Him as a chalice would with the sea.

The unheralded character of God's coming is matched only by the completeness with which one is overwhelmed by God's very being, as the chalice we place on our altar would be overwhelmed if it were placed in the sea. Death means being placed in God (like a chalice might be placed in the sea) and being overwhelmed by God's love. Death means being placed in Love.

Being in love with another human being is surely one of the healthiest and happiest experiences that can happen to us in this life. Being in love transforms an ordinary prosaic life suddenly into poetry. It is an experience that brings insights, intuitions, blessings that before one never even realized could exist.

Imagine what it must be, not simply to be in love with someone, but to be in Love. Period. In God who is love. Immersed in this transcendent Love, we find ourselves in God and experience the joyous reality that we are one with God.

Sr. Theresa Daniel, who loved so many people during her mortal life – her family, her friends, her sisters, her students, so many people -- has discovered – what all of us will someday discover--that, quite literally, SHE IS –IN LOVE.

SR. MADELINE THERESE KELSO 10-29-1998

Readings: 1 Cor. 13:1-13
Jn. 15:9-16

The day that Sr. Madeline Therese died I was in Cincinnati. One afternoon I yielded to temptation and visited a book store. I emerged poorer financially, richer intellectually. One of the books I bought was a translation of the autobiography of St. Therese: *The Story of a Soul.* I was really searching for the real Therese of Lisieux, for I understand that her autobiography had been "doctored up" by her sisters. They had removed anything that might disedify readers.

I have always had a kind of love-hate relationship with her. I was both put off by her story, yet fascinated by it. Put off by what seemed to be a saccharine sentimentality: she was too sweet, too pious. I wondered to myself: what would she say if she stubbed her toe or slipped on a patch of ice? I found myself almost hoping that it wouldn't be a prayer, that at least she would say: darn. Maybe even something stronger. I wanted her to act in such situations as I would act. And I doubt that prayer would be my first immediate reaction to such mishaps.

Yet even while I was put off by her language, I found myself fascinated by the obvious strength of heart and clarity of mind that seemed always to possess her. And I realized that the piety of the late 19th century was very different from the spirituality of the late 20th century. Making allowances for that difference, I admired her strength of character and simplicity of purpose. She knew who she was. She had a deep sense of herself. There were no masks. She simply was who she was. And once one gets beyond the somewhat drippy sentimentality that holy people in her time were expected to express, it is possible to get to know her as the real person she truly was – and is so transparently – before God.

It's interesting that, though she lived most of her short life behind cloister walls, one of her great heroines was Joan of Arc, who was not exactly a stay-at-home person. She can easily be linked, too, with some of the great saints of the early Christian period: the martyrs, for it was her desire to join them in their total gift of themselves to God. She wanted to carry out heroic deeds for Jesus: "I feel in myself the courage of the crusader…I would want to die in battle in defense of the Church." She was canonized 25 years after her death: very brief interstices indeed. I have to say that she might not have made it in our day, as she said quite definitively: "I feel in me the vocation of the

Priest." That wouldn't go over big in today's Church! Yet she tells us that, in imitation of the humility of St. Francis of Assisi, she also felt the vocation of imitating him in refusing the sublime dignity of the priesthood (p. 192).

Yes, the more you read St. Therese, the more you come to admire the steely courage and the marvelous humanity that even the sentimental piety of a bygone age cannot conceal.

You may wonder why I am saying so much about St. Therese of the Child Jesus, when we gather here to give Sr. Madeline Therese back to God. My first reason is that she would want it this way. She loved Therese in life and surely with greater love now in the wondrous community of saints. She would want me to talk about her beloved patron.

Second, I talk about St. Therese because I believe that many elements of her story are duplicated in the life of Sr. Madeline Therese. Sr. Madeline Therese was a pious person, living a piety that many could not identify with or even understand. Yet it was not a surface piety: it had deep roots and those roots, like those of St. Therese, are to be found in the Gospel. The two scripture readings for this evening inspired the two Thereses whom we are remembering tonight in this liturgy.

In that last quarter of the 19th century when St. Therese lived, the liturgy had ceased to be the source and fount of the true Christian spirit. It was a liturgy without participation. Therese a Carmelite nun, was not even allowed to receive communion each day. The only source of the true Christian spirit available to her was the Scriptures. She tells us that it was in this Book of Life that she found the way in which God was calling her. She was reading First Corinthians looking for her way to God. She read chapter 12 which speaks of various offices in the Church, apostles, administrators, prophets, doctors and the rest. She knew that none of these was for her. Then she went on to that moving 13th chapter which speaks of love as the MOST EXCELLENT WAY. Her vocation, she realized, was LOVE. "Love," she wrote, "comprises all vocations. Love is everything. It embraces all times and places. In a word it is eternal."

St. Therese also read this evening's Gospel and saw even more deeply into the Christian vocation of love. For love was Jesus' command, His special command. She thrilled to the recognition that it was no longer simply loving one's neighbor as oneself, but loving the neighbor as Jesus loved the neighbor and will love till the end of the world.

If St. Therese found her "little way" in the scriptures, Sr. Madeline Therese found that same way in St. Therese's life story. The whole intent of her life was to live this way of spiritual childhood. She took delight in her work at Nazareth in the Education Department and in the speech clinic. She taught young women and men how to teach children. She was happy in doing this. And she was wonderfully adept in helping young children in remedial reading. Something she truly love to do and did so very well. From her teaching, students learned reading skills they would use later in their own teaching. From contact with her person, they learned something much more precious: not just how to read or teach reading, but how to live as authentic persons. They learned to be more loving, caring persons, and they learned this because they saw it so clearly in her.

As we give her back to God, we do so with the confidence that her way of life has led her to God and to her dear patron. We remember her as a holy person. We may not always want to imitate the externals of her piety. (I wonder how many people here she induced to say the novena to St. Therese?). But beyond those externals was a depth of spiritual wealth that perhaps not everyone fully appreciated while she was in our midst. That was the real Madeline Therese; the true self that she was –and is now so transparently --before God.

Now she belongs to the heavenly communion of saints. On Sunday we shall celebrate that communion, and remember that she and all the blessed are cheering us on, as we journey through life on our way to enter fully into communion with her and all God's holy ones.

SISTERS IN VARIOUS MINISTRIES

SR. AGATHA CORGEL 2-16-2005

Wis. 3:1-6,9
2 Cor., 4:14-18;5:1
Jn. 14: 1-6

I got to know Sr. Agatha in what would probably be
called her declining years. I am not sure, though, that I
would want to call those last years "declining. For while it
is true, as Paul puts it, that "our outer nature is wasting
away," nevertheless –again to quote Paul –"our inner
nature is being renewed day by day." Anyway, however we

choose to describe those later years of her life, it was in those years that I came to know Sr. Agatha: the years when her inner nature was being renewed day by day. Curiously, we met in the old community room at 4095 East Avenue. One day, when I came to get my mail, she was sitting in the community room. I went over to say hello to her. That began a relationship that went on for some time and always in the same context. Day after day as I came to pick up my mail, Agatha was waiting in the community room for my greeting. There were no lengthy conversations, just a brief exchange of greetings. Each day she waited for me to come.

Finally, when her deteriorating physical health meant going to the Infirmary, she faced a different kind of waiting. In the Gospel Jesus speaks of going to prepare a place for you, then (He said) I will come and bring you to be with me. It seemed as if Jesus was never coming to get her and bring her home as he had promised. She had to wait. We might want to ask today: why all this fruitless period of waiting?

Let's talk about that. Was it fruitless? As her contact with the outward world was lessening, she was, in a way that we cannot understand, living at the level of the unconscious. That is an area of human life that most of us know very little about. We encounter it at times in dreams; and, as we all know strange experiences can take place in those unconscious moments when we are dreaming. Thomas Merton once wrote to a correspondent what I think was a very perceptive statement. He said: "We are too rational. We do not permit anything to remain unconscious. Yet all that is best is unconscious or superconscious." (*The Hidden Ground of* Love, 341).

Whatever was going on in Sr. Agatha in those years we cannot know. We can believe though that, as conscious distractions were removed, she was in contact with God more completely than she had ever been -- and in a way we cannot understand. And at some point she passed into that liminal stage, where she was no longer in this world, yet not yet fully in the next. In this in-between stage, she was at the threshold of heavenly joy and bliss, as Christ –at last true to his promise to come for her – was leading her into the joy and peace of her heavenly home.

What can Sr. Agatha's life teach us? One theme we can perhaps learn from her life is the value of waiting. We need to learn the meaning of waiting. We live in a hurried, frenzied culture, in which waiting is an inconvenience we feel we simply have to put up with. We wait impatiently in a traffic line because there is an accident up ahead. We wait in line at Wegman's because there were so many insensitive people who decided to shop at the same time we did. We wait in an airport for a plane that has been delayed for several hours. So much of life is waiting and so often we see it as nothing but frustration.

Yet there is another kind of waiting. A mother waiting for her child to be born. Waiting for a son or daughter or a niece or nephew to grow up to the maturity that the brightness of youth promises. There is the waiting for the right answer to a question, as I begin to grasp the elements of the question and as my struggle moves me in the direction of an answer; but for the fullness of that answer I shall have to wait. These are examples of the kinds of waiting that bring not frustration, but the joy of anticipated expectation. The joy of expectation participates in the joy of fulfillment. Part of the joy of a journey is preparing for it.

Waiting is the characteristic stance of the liturgical season of Advent. We await the Lord's coming with the realization that he is already in our midst; yet, since we are not fully aware of his presence, we have to wait for our consciousness to catch up with reality. Waiting is living with the mystery that is to come. But before it can come we have to wait.

There is a poem by R. S. Thomas, Anglican priest and Welsh poet, called "Kneeling." He pictures himself kneeling before an altar just before he is to preach. There is silence in the air like a staircase from heaven. Sunlight plays upon the preacher as he is about to become God's spokesperson. He asks God to prompt him in what he says; yet he realizes all too well – as every preacher must – that, even though God speaks through him, something will be lost. People will have to wait. It takes time for God's meaning to sink into their hearts. But the meaning will emerge from the waiting:

> Moments of calm,
> Kneeling before an altar
> Of wood in a stone church
> In summer, waiting for the God
> To speak; the air a staircase
> For silence; the sun's light
> Ringing me, as though I acted
> A great role...
> [The listeners] waiting, as I,
> For the message.
> Prompt me God,
> but not yet. When I speak,
> Though it be you who speak
> Through me, something is lost.
> The meaning is in the waiting.

The long waiting of Agatha's life is over. The waiting was meaningful. For it opened her heart and mind to the meaning of the Gospel: of the Lord's coming to take her home to himself. This aspect of her life can teach us that there can be meaning in waiting. Waiting can put us in touch with the mystery of our existence and help prepare us as we continue our pilgrim journey toward our heavenly home.

Sr. Albertus Schauseil 2-15-2005

Readings: Wis. 7:24-28
1 Cor. 13: 1-3
Lk. 11: 28-42

Thursday evening, the evening before she died, I was in Sr. Albertus's room. Mary Jane Mitchell was there too. I caught up with Mary Jane afterwards and said to her: "Dying is hard. It's not easy to die. But this is a great place to do it. Here you never die alone. You are surrounded by loved ones. You are embraced by love."

I thought about this later and I am sure that there is an important truth in what I said. Yet, as I reflected, it seemed clear to me that, at a deeper level, it must be said that each one of us dies alone. There is, if you will, a liminal stage between dying and death. It is the threshold of eternity, where one takes leave of this mortal life, without yet having entered fully into eternal life. It's a stage of inwardness, where we lose contact with our surroundings and our loved ones. We are alone -- yet not really alone, for the Risen Jesus is at our side and it is He who finally leads us across that threshold into the life of eternal joy and peace. Some are in that liminal stage for only a short time. But for many, as I think it was for Albertus, it can be a protracted period of time. Friday morning she crossed that threshold into the fullness of the communion of saints, where Mother Agnes Cecilia and a host of other SSJs surely awaited her.

Three months ago to the day –November 15 – we celebrated the feast of St. Albert the Great. Then, as each year, Sr. Albertus always enjoyed my announcing her feast day as the feast of Sr. Albertus the Great. In many wonderful ways she was Albertus the Great. On any count she was a truly remarkable woman. As I think of her, I remember the well-known words of Oliver Goldsmith in his poem "The Deserted Village":

> And still they gazed, and still the wonder grew
> That one small head could carry all she knew.

We might want to add: that one small office could contain all the stuff that she accumulated over the course of the years.

She was small in stature, it's true, but her head carried more than you could ever get into the most recent computer. She more than earned her title: "All-purpose Al."

It was like earning a Ph. D. in how to do almost anything. As everyone knows, "All-purpose Al" knew every pipe, every bit of wiring, all the nuts and bolts in the Motherhouse at 4095 East Avenue. One of her special projects was the chapel sound system. Hardly anything went on at the Motherhouse Chapel that she didn't get on tape and she was ever eager to share her growing number of tapes with anyone who showed the slightest interest. And many a person is grateful to her for that sharing. In fact, she was never hesitant about sharing with others, not only her tapes, but her enormous fund of knowledge. One thing for sure, she was never lost for words. And she talked with her forefinger.

Last night after the wake, I found that the first copies of my book, HERE on the Way to THERE: A Catholic Reflection on Dying and What Follows had arrived from the publisher. So, not surprising, last night I had a dream about Sr. Albertus. She appeared to me and said: "Your book is pretty good. But let me tell you what the real thing is like." This she proceeded to do. Suddenly it was 6:30 a.m. and my alarm clock went off; and, you know, even after I woke up, she kept on talking.

Sr. Albertus did not choose readings for her funeral liturgy. So I chose as the Gospel for her: the narrative about Martha and her sister Mary. It's an appropriate one for her. Jesus' words to Martha, "You are busy about many things," surely fit our Albertus. Anyone at the Motherhouse could detail those many things she was busy about. She was a walking blue-print of the Motherhouse. Compared to what hers was, my office is a model of order and neatness. Her office was a vision to behold: organized chaos. She could find anything there: a button, a screw, a pair of pliers, a screwdriver, a piece of cloth (whatever color you needed). Once I believe I saw a "Vote for Herbert Hoover" button there. Well, maybe I am exaggerating a bit, but you have to admit this was by no means beyond the realm of possibility. She was great at sewing. Each year as I lost another inch in height, she would shorten the chasuble by an inch. (Who is going to do that now or must I dare not lose another inch?) She was most faithful in reading the Bible each day – and also the Wall Street Journal

If you read the story of Martha and Mary carefully, it is very clear that Martha is by far the stronger of the two women. It's a story that all too often has been woefully misinterpreted. It has absolutely nothing to say about the active life and the contemplative life (though it has often been exploited for that purpose, especially by monastic people, like Bernard of Clairvaux, for instance). In reality it's a simple story: two sisters, obviously dear to Jesus, extending hospitality to him. Each offers hospitality in her own way: Martha by preparing a meal for Jesus, Mary by keeping him company. It's a quiet, peaceful scene, momentarily marred by Martha's quite reasonable complaint directed against her sister. At this point Jesus gently suggests to Martha to stop fussing over the meal. It's as if he is saying: "I'm here to enjoy your company, not to test your culinary skills." Jesus is teasing Martha: "Stop sweating it, Martha. A snack will do. Come on over here and chat with us. That's the hospitality I want: to be able to share with you and Mary. I have been talking here with Mary, but I want you in on the visit too. That is the much better thing for you to do. Mary has done it already." And the story ends happily with all three enjoying one another's company. It's a delightful story of Jesus experiencing the joys of human friendship.

Like Martha, Albertus was a strong woman and an impressive one too. She showed a strength that came from a deep and calm sense of knowing what she was doing and why. She had a sense of purpose in life and a deep commitment to mission. Yes, she knew all the nuts and bolts of the Motherhouse, but that knowledge was not for herself. It was knowledge she could put to good purpose for the life of the community and the Congregation. What she knew was not just knowledge. It was wisdom -- knowledge directed toward God's purposes and the good of others.

She realized that, in the long run, it wasn't knowledge that mattered so much as love. She knew in the living out of her own religious vocation the importance of Paul's words: "If I have all knowledge, but do not have love, I am nothing." That is why she was always eager to do things for people. Love was her motive. One of the things I marveled about in her was the fact that when she did do something for you, she gave you the impression that she was grateful to you for letting her do it for you.

What would Albertus want us to remember from her life? Perhaps this: Three things abide: faith, hope and love, but the greatest of these is love.

SR. MARY WEAVER 9-9-2004

Readings: Is. 25:6-9
1Cor. 15: 53-58
Mt. 25: 31, 34-40

It was a unique and holy moment to be in her room when Sr. Mary Weaver died. It was particularly a holy and grace-filled moment for Mary Paul and Kathleen Klier who had keep vigil so lovingly at her side for so long a time. In retrospect, as Mary took her last breath, I thought of the angel at Jesus' tomb. It was as if the angel was saying to those of us who were in the room: "Don't look for her here any longer. She has gone. She has been raised. She has returned to God who made her."

And the angel would say she, not her soul, but she, Mary the person. It is surely our greatest joy to realize that it was in the totality of her personhood that Mary has been raised and has returned to God. She has put off her mortal body and put on an immortal body. What a joy for her and a source of rejoicing for us. She who replaced broken cars with new ones has put off her old body that suffered so much in those last weeks and put on a new body.

This is what Paul is talking about in that rather mysterious second reading from first Corinthians where he insists that this perishable body must put on imperishability, this mortal body must put on immortality.

For, whether we are living in this life or have, like Mary, entered into new life, it isn't that we *have* bodies; we *are* bodies. Always the human person is an embodied person. Mary now is an embodied person. And the wonderful thing about it is that it's a body that will never get cold. No need any more for layers of sweaters.

The Gospel applies so perfectly to Mary whose whole life was one of caring for others, whether that caring meant getting them cars -- or food or clothing or housing, didn't matter. The Gospel and its link with Mary reminds me of a wonderful book by Mitch Albom, called **The Five People You Meet in Heaven**.

The book is about a man named Eddie. Eddie spends most of his life as maintenance man at an amusement park. His job is to protect the lives of the park's visitors by making sure that everything, especially the cars on the various rides, is in best repair. On his eighty-third birthday he dies in a tragic accident trying to save a little girl from a falling cart on one of the rides in the amusement park.

In heaven he meets the five people – loved ones and strangers – who entered into and most affected his life. In heaven, he is told "you get to make sense of your yesterdays" (92).

The book ends with a kind of apocalyptic scene, in which at the pier of the amusement park, thousands of people, men and women, fathers and mothers and children fill the board walk, the beaches, the rides – all people who were there because of the simple, mundane things Eddie had done in his life, the accidents he prevented, the cars he had kept safe. Eddie is astonished. They are all there to honor him. Then in the midst of this huge gathering he sees a woman approaching him with her arms extended. It's his wife. He reaches for her and he sees her smile and both their voices melt into a single word: ***Home***.

I was struck by how much this story is a kind of pale version of Mary's story. In her last years -- here at the Motherhouse -- she took cars for repair so that all of us would be safe. But before that – in Alabama, the place where her heart always remained --, she cared for the poor, the hungry, the homeless, the needy. She gave of herself without thinking of the cost. What she gave she gave – not because she thought of any gain, temporal or eternal – she gave simply because what she gave was needed. That was all that mattered to Mary. There was nothing spectacular about her way of life. She chose to live a simple life just giving of herself.

That is why we can imagine she got the surprise of her life as the Gospel story was reenacted before her very eyes -- as she saw multitudes giving testimony for her: hundreds of us and many more hundreds of the hungry, the poor, the sick, the homeless, the needy whom she touched wherever she went. All of us and all of these people were saying to God: "Yes, we were in need and she took care of us. We were poor and hungry and she took care of us. We were homeless and sick and despondent and she took care of us."

Then in wonderment she heard the voice of Jesus: "Mary, insofar as you did all this to the least of my sisters and brothers, you did it to me."

And Eddie, remember, was met by a woman who had been waiting for him. Can anyone doubt that Mary, as she entered into heaven, was also welcomed by a woman who had been waiting for her? And who else but her twin sister, Perpetua? And in one voice they said: "*Home.*" Home together – Perpetua and Felicitas. Or rather Ann and Mary are once again together – as they will be for all eternity.

She is no longer Felicitas in name (she gave that up as soon as she could), but she is felicitas in reality. For felicitas means blessedness, happiness, and that is what heaven is all about: complete and total happiness.

Yesterday, as I was going from chapel to the dining room, I took special note of the Alabama window. It shows Jesus blessing the poor and the disabled, especially the children. But if you look intently with the eyes of faith, I think you can see in the figure of Jesus also the features of Mary Weaver. For it was in her and through her that Jesus was able to care for so many people, even though Mary probably never stopped to think of it that way. She was too busy doing what needed to be done.

If there is a place in heaven for the unpretentious and the lowly -- that's the place Mary will choose to be. Actually, it's the best place to be. For, remember, another woman named Mary knew that so very well. That is why she did not hesitate to say that God's penchant is to look with favor on his **lowly** servant, God's penchant is to bring down the mighty and lift up the **lowly**. That is what Mary of Nazareth in Galilee said and that is what Mary of Nazareth in Pittsford truly believed and lived.

Mary of Nazareth in Galilee, pray for us.
Mary of Nazareth in Pittsford, pray for us.

SR. IMELDA WUEST 6-25-2004

Readings: Is. 60:19-20, 22
Philippians 3: 7-12
Lk. 9: 22-28

I remember five years ago the funeral Mass of Mary Wuest. I recall speaking of her gracious and tender love for Imelda and the love they both had for Fr. Ray. I have a gold nail clip that once belonged to Ray that they gave me and I cherish it still as a remembrance of all three of them. We are here today to celebrate the fact that Sr. Imelda has –at long last – joined Mary and Ray in the wondrous joy of the fullness of life with God.

Her gifts were many. I understand that she was a fabulously good teacher, and especially for little children. A happy, joyous person, she loved a good time – and a good card game. She was a person of great generosity, as so many people have testified. Yet I dare say that her gifts were those of a unique group of people, namely, those who choose to live in the background. She never had the slightest desire to be the star of the show. She was quite content to play a supporting role. This is a rare gift. There was a humility about Imelda that you had to admire and only wish you could imitate. It is so easy for us to center life around ourselves. When we do this we forget one fundamental fact of human existence: namely, that with one relatively unimportant exception, the world is made up of other people. Humility is the only safeguard against a mentality of self-centeredness. True humility prevents us from taking ourselves too seriously or worrying too much about what others may think of us. It was that kind of self-forgetfulness that made Imelda a woman who was truly free. She was free just to be herself without any pretending to be anything more. This meant she was able to be free for others.

I had never heard of St. Imelda. So out of curiosity I decided to look up her life. I was sorry I did: it's a weird story. She lived in the 14th century in the city of Bologna -- a young Italian girl, Imelda Lambertini. From childhood she longed to receive Holy Communion. On one occasion in particular she was in Church, earnestly wanting to receive the sacrament, but she could not because she was only eleven and at that time children were not allowed to receive till the age of 14. This particular day she prayed with breaking heart to God that she might receive communion. Suddenly the tabernacle door swung open. A host flew out, sailed over the pews till it came to 11 year old Imelda and just remained there hovering over her head. The priest, bewildered by what he saw, decided this must be a sign that he had better give communion to her. So he did. In a rapturous ecstasy of love and joy, as she received the Lord she had so ardently desired to receive, Imelda died on the spot. That's the story!

Pretty weird bit of hagiography, isn't it? Everything so easy for her. For our dear, little Imelda things were not so easy. Happily she didn't have St. Imelda's problem about communion. Our resident saint (and I don't use that term lightly) Fr. Bruce so thoughtfully and lovingly brought her communion every day. But no dying in rapturous ecstasy for our Imelda. Instead, she had to live the truth of today's Gospel: followers of Jesus have to take up the cross daily and follow him. The Gospel paradox is that the only way we can save ourselves in by losing ourselves. True growth as a disciple of Jesus comes, not from hanging on, but from letting go.

Imelda's life became a life of letting go. When she let go of teaching, she became one of the Motherhouse drivers. She enjoyed this ministry, but the time came that she had to give up driving. I can testify --and there are others here too who can testify -- that that is a major letting go in life. Blessed are those who can do it graciously. But there were other lettings go that Imelda had to endure: letting go of her independence as she moved to the Infirmary. As time went on she had to let go of her ability to communicate with people in any substantive way. And as her health failed critically, but life lingered on and on, she had to let go of her desire to leave this life and be with her loved ones in God. The final letting go came on Tuesday when she let go of this earthly existence and exchanged it for an immortal life in the loving embrace of God.

This funeral liturgy is more for us than for Imelda. She participates now in a glorious liturgy of which our best liturgical celebrations are but dim shadows. What can we learn from this celebration of her entry into God? What would she want to say to us today? I know it is presumptuous of me, but I am going to try to tell you what I think she might want to say. I suggest there might be two things:

First, do learn the wisdom of learning when and how "to let go." I learned it the hard way. I wish I had learned it earlier. Don't let yourself be tied to a past that is rapidly receding. Don't hang on to what is no longer life-giving. Have the courage to live in the present and to move on to whatever the future holds out to you. Listen carefully to the words Paul addressed to the Philippians: "Forgetting what lies behind, I press on toward what lies ahead" (3:14).

The second thing she might say to you could be something like this. "I know that my situation in the last several years was the cause of concern to many of you. To put it bluntly, you wondered why God made me linger on and on. Why did God make me suffer for so long? Why didn't God take me earlier? And maybe a second question: Where was God in all of this? I have to admit I had some of these questions myself.

"I understand now and I will try to explain it to you. I am not sure you will be able to grasp it, at least with the fullness of the understanding I now have. But let me try. The thinking behind those questions seems to be that God is in charge of the universe God made and is able to make changes whenever God chooses to do so. But that isn't really the way things are. In an act of divine love God created the universe. The glory of that universe is that God made human beings with free will. God respects that free will. He persuades it, but he never attempts to dominate it. Besides creating women and men who were free, God also created a universe with its own autonomy. God respects

- 147 -

that autonomy. The universe follows its own inner directions which God does not choose to interfere with.

"I know this is getting a bit heavy. In fact, I probably sound like a theologian. Actually where I am, I know more than all your theologians put together, as I see the face of God. I will try to put it quite simply. God is not a puppeteer. He is not pulling strings that determine the way everything happens. God is not a master chess player moving all the figures around as He/She wills. Rather, God respects the integrity of all that God made.

Indeed, I might say *God's refusal to tinker with the universe God created is a supreme act of letting go.* Out of love for the integrity of the universe God lets go of control – a control that would suffocate, a control that would overwhelm. In a wonderful act of love and trust God. let the universe be free to be itself.

"As to the other question: Where was God in all of this? That's a question I knew the answer to all along. I just was no longer able to communicate it to you. Where was God? God was right there with me all along. God was comforting me, strengthening me, loving me. But of course you probably never saw it, as God was doing it from within. After all, that is where God is. God is in all of us. God is in you. But you have to open yourselves to the discovery of God's presence. That is my invitation to you. In the meantime, keep praying – not so much for me or to me but with me."

SR. BARBARA HUGHES 6-19-2004

Readings: Rev.:22: 1-5
1 Cor. 12:27-31; 13:1-2, 8-13
Jn, 11:20-27

Barbara, can you hear me now?

I have a number of images of Sr. Barbara that come to mind. The most recent and the most poignant was seeing her sitting in front of the nurses' station, a bit hunched-over, looking intently down the corridor – even though she could not see anything that was going on. One occasion I especially remember. I pulled up by her in my cart and greeted her. She recognized my voice, but she said: "All I can see before me is a form. I can't make out any of the features of a person." She went on to say: "But it's all right. "Whatever God wants." That was almost a mantra on her part: "whatever God wants." I refrained from saying to her that I didn't think God wanted her to be blind. All I could do was to think to myself: How wonderful the gift she was ready to give to God: not her blindness, but her acceptance of a most difficult loss, an acceptance that was wholehearted. An acceptance of darkness, of an on-going night, even though there was light all around. She was more than resigned. She was content. "Whatever God wants" covered everything.

Now Barbara is truly experiencing what God really wants for her. As that wonderful reading from Revelation makes clear, she now sees the face of God. No more darkness for her. No more night. She will need no light or lamp to see. For God who is the fullness of light will be the light in which she will see everything. Right now, at this very time she sees us and she sees us in God. For whether we realize it or not, that is where we are. Where else could we be?

I want to return to the occasion I mentioned earlier when I went to see Barbara. I gave her a blessing and then asked her to pray over me. She raised her hand over me and spoke a healing message. The message was at least a good sized paragraph long and she said it rapidly. It was not something she was making up. It was a language that I did not recognize at all. I realized that she was speaking in tongues. Speaking in tongues was a phenomenon in the early church. It is attested to by St. Paul in the reading we heard from 1st Corinthians, as one of the gifts of the Spirit.

Sr. Barbara never simply spoke in tongues: it was always connected with healing. She felt strongly that God had given her the power to heal. And she used that power lavishly. I wonder how many doctors and dentists and nurses between Mt. Morris and Rochester and environs have suddenly been surprised by a healing prayer said over them by a sometimes loquacious nun. She always insisted, though, that one had to have faith: one had to believe that God was working through her or there would be no healing.

She herself was a woman of great faith. I think of her as a strong woman of faith – like Martha in our Gospel. Mary and Martha are so often compared, with Martha coming out second best. Yet it is clear from the Gospels that Martha is by far the stronger woman of the two. Indeed in our Gospel reading, she makes one of the most profound expressions of faith in Jesus in the entire New Testament. Her profession far outstrips that of Peter at Caesarea Philippi.

Yet Barbara knew, as Paul makes so clear in our second reading, that all the gifts of the Spirit pale in significance to the most excellent of all the gifts: the gift of God's love. Barbara experienced that love during her life. But as her life was drawing to its earthly end (and she knew that's what was happening), Barbara was no longer content to live simply in the shadows of God's love. She wanted to live in the fullness of God's love. She expressed this by saying she wanted to die. But that desire to die must be translated. It needs to be translated into the way St. Paul expressed the same desire: "For me living is Christ and dying is gain." (Philippians 1:21) It takes us a lifetime to come to this realization. Someone has said: life is what we do while we are waiting to die. That's not quite right. Our earthly life is important and we need to live it to the fullest. But there is in all of us, even when we don't realize it, a yearning that we cannot always identify completely. Barbara knows, as we cannot yet know, that that yearning will never be satisfied till we enter into the full embrace of God's Love.

Barbara, I am sorry I can't play the bagpipes and I don't dare sing Loch Lomond, but I do have the words of a traditional song of Scotland that I want to read. It is called "The End of the Road."

Ev'ry road thro'life is a long, long
>road,
>Filled with joys and sorrows too
>As you journey on how your heart will yearn
>For the things most dear to you.
>With wealth and love 'tis so,
>But onward we must go.
>>Chorus:
Keep right on to the end of the road,
>>Keep right on to the end,
>Tho' the way be long, let your heart be strong.
>>Keep right on round the bend.
>Tho' you're tired and weary, still journey on,
>>Till you come to your happy abode
>Where all the love you've been dreaming of,
>>Will be there at the end of the road.

SR. PAUL MARGARET 3-1-2004

Readings: Deut. 7: 6-9
Philippians 1: 8-11
Mt. 11: 25-30

As most of you know, I have been a member (or quasi-member, if you want to be legalistic about it) of the Congregation of the Sisters of St. Joseph since 1946. Whenever the Sisters renew their commitment to the Congregation, I skip the first part that has to do with the vows and join (quietly) in the second part which says in substance: "I want to live and die in the Congregation of the Sisters of St. Joseph." For me, living among the Sisters of St. Joseph has been very good (generally at least); but what is more important to me is dying as a member (or quasi-member, if you insist) of the Sisters of St. Joseph.

Dying in this house is a *holy moment*, as you experience a person (whether conscious or not) making her final act of freedom, saying her ultimate Yes to God. It is a *holy moment* because one who dies here is always surrounded in those dying moments by people who care, people who love, people who pray. It is a *holy moment* because the more than 900 sisters who have already said their final Yes to God in years gone by are also in that room praying and readying a welcome for the new arrival. And at 9:05 p.m. Wednesday, February 26, guess who was at their head – at that holy moment last Wednesday night -- to welcome Sr. Paul Margaret? Sr. Irene, of course. Irene has been waiting for her and now they are together again, as it always was.

Sr. Paul Margaret herself chose the readings for this Mass and, further, gave orders that she wanted the Mass of the Sacred Heart. The readings she chose are interesting. The first, from Deuteronomy, expresses God's love for God's people. It is a love that is truly love, but a love that is distant. For it is the love of a God whom people do not fully understand. It's a love they are not always quite sure of. For this God is one who loves His people, yet at times seems to want to punish them for their sins.

The readings from the Gospel and from the Epistle to the Philippians are also about God, but a God whose love is a very different kind of love. It is a love that has come near to us. For it is a Love that has become incarnate. It is only with the Incarnation that God is able to love us with a human heart, which is to say, in a way that we can understand. Only a God with a human heart can say to us: "Come to me with your burdens and sufferings and I will give you rest. For I know the limitations and the hardships than being human is heir to, for I have experienced them. I am the compassion of God that St. Paul speaks of in the reading from Philippians. I love you with a human heart."

It was out of this context that devotion developed in the Church to the Sacred Heart as the symbol of God's love – a love that Deuteronomy could never express. By making the rather unusual request that her funeral Mass be the Mass of the Sacred Heart, Sr. Paul Margaret was intending to draw us to a deeper love of the Sacred Heart, which so obviously was an important part of her spiritual life.

As I speak to you, I wonder what your attitude is toward devotion to the Sacred Heart. Some people have been put off by this devotion. Put off, in large part perhaps, by some of the images of the Sacred Heart that have so often accompanied this devotion. They show a Christ who looks effeminate and even sexless. Images of this sort, far from bringing him closer to us, seemed to distance us from Him. It is hard to see true humanity in Him.

I doubt if it was this frail, almost alien image of Jesus that Sr. Paul Margaret had in mind. The Christ of the Sacred Heart that she knew was the strong, courageous Christ who really is on fire with love for us. His is a strong human love than is transformed by the divine. For it is nothing less than God's love embodied in One who is truly human. I suspect this may be what those images hoped to present, but many people found it difficult to see them in that way.

In a religious context, images are very important to us in conveying religious and spiritual truths. Good images can open up the meaning of a religious truth. Bad images can obscure that meaning. All too many images of the

Sacred Heart have tended to obscure rather than reveal God's love incarnate in Someone who was fully human.

At a time when violence seems to meet us whatever way we turn, the image of the Sacred Heart has a strong potential for informing a spirituality of nonviolence. For it symbolizes a love that shows a willingness to take suffering on oneself rather than inflict harm on another. And that is what nonviolence is all about: a readiness to suffer for the truth, the truth that eventually can become the common ground of friend and foe alike. For nonviolence seeks to turn foes into friends through self-sacrificing love.

When a sister picks out her own readings for her funeral, intentionally or not, she is choosing to teach us through these readings. Sr. Paul Margaret chose readings that she hoped would help us grasp the full and true meaning of devotion to the Sacred Heart. The courageous and loving God, incarnate in the One we call Lord – this, I believe, is the strong image of the Sacred Heart, This, I believe, is what she wants us to grasp.

I say this because she was an unusual sort of person. There was a sturdy gentleness about her. I always admired the obvious confidence she revealed on the days she chose to read the first reading at Mass. She took her time coming up to the lectern and with an appropriate sense of self-assurance truly proclaimed the scripture in a way that invited you to listen.

Today we listen to the readings she chose and surely it is only right to see them as her final gift to us. May she rest in peace in the heart of her God.

SR. VIRGINIA MAHANEY 10-23-2003

Readings: Is. 43: 1-5
Acts 2:25-28
Jn. 14: 1-6

As some of you know, I am writing a book about death, dying and new life. The title I have chosen for the book is "Where Do We Go From Here?" Last Saturday I had dinner at a Chinese restaurant and at the end of the meal the waiter gave me the customary fortune cookie. In the light of the title I had given to my book I was a bit startled to read the little paper inside. It said: "You are almost there."

That small bit of paper became a source of fruitful meditation for me. It reminded me of the mortality of our lives. Each of us could really be told: "You are almost there." No matter how long we have to live our mortal lives, it is but a brief period compared to the immortal existence that awaits us.

If this is true of all of us, it is especially true of people who have a terminal illness. Twelve years ago, Sr. Virginia was told by her physician that she had cancer and eventually she was told that there was nothing medical science could do for her. For twelve years, she experienced (in a way most of us don't) that she was "almost there." She was a very private person and hardly anyone knew how serious her condition was. She faced her future with a wonderful courage and a sense of peace.

We may ask: how did she do it? What was the source of this undauntable courage that she had? How could she face so dark a future with an outlook that was so bright, and hope-filled? The answer to that question we can never know for sure, as it was something between herself and her God – a relationship that none of us was privy to. Perhaps, though, we can look for some plausible answers in the readings she chose for her funeral liturgy. When a person chooses the readings for her funeral service or has dear friends choose them for her, it is not a happenstance thing. It is, I believe, the grace of God guiding these choices and telling us what she wants us to hear.

One of the insights that comes through loud and clear in the readings is her sense of personal union with God. She was convinced that God loved her, that her whole being was enfolded in that divine love. She knew that God was with her, no matter where she was and what happened to her. Why do I say that? Because, as the first reading says, she is precious in God's eyes and she truly believed it.

That is something that is true of all of us; yet we don't reflect on it enough. Sr. Virginia chose that text because she really believed it. She realized that she was indeed precious in God's eyes, not so much because of anything she had done, but because God had redeemed her and saved her. It is a wonderful thing to **know** that we are precious in God's eyes, that we are indeed loved by God; but it is so easy to let these wonderful truths remain just speculative knowledge that we hold in our minds, but not always in our hearts. A truth that is in our heads but not in our hearts has little influence on the way we live our lives.

Sr. Virgina not only knew how precious she was to God, that God loved her, but —what is much more wonderful-- she **experienced** that love with joy and with a sense of certitude that brooked no doubts. Surely it was that experience that kept her going and cheerful, despite the pain and suffering she endured. Indeed, I am sure that if she were here in my place today, she might want to put to each one of us the question: Do you really believe that you are precious to God, that you are loved by God with a love that surpasses all understanding? Are you ready, as I was, to stake your whole life on that belief?

Another insight from the readings is her conviction that she was on the final stage of an irreversible journey to God and in that journey, without her always knowing how, God was leading her toward that journey's goal. God was at her side. As the second reading says: "You will not abandon me. For you have made known to me the ways of life." And if the journey was sometimes through the valley of darkness, God was still at her side pumping into her a joy that only those who are close to God can truly experience. As the reading says: "You have filled me with the joy of your presence."

The Gospel suggests to me that Sr. Virginia looked forward to her death as a homecoming. Jesus, as the Gospel tells us, had gone ahead – to make ready for her coming. The last words I heard Sr. Virginia speak were the words that conclude the Bible, as they concluded her life. The words were: "Come, Lord Jesus, come!" Last Wednesday Jesus came. He came to bring her home – to her only true home. He came to fulfill the promise of the Gospel: "I shall come and take you with me, that where I am you also may be." What a holy moment it was –the moment Virginia took her last breath and Jesus was there to claim her as his own.

Yet, when all is said and done, a funeral liturgy is more for the living than for those who have died. They have passed through death to eternal joy. We, the living, still have that passage to make. Sr. Virginia is "already there" – experiencing the fullness of heaven's joys. And all of us, no matter what age we may be, are, in one way or another, "almost there." Thus a liturgy of this kind moves us to reflect on our own mortality: not with fear or anxiety, but with faith and hope in God's wondrous concern for us. We can look at death and be prepared to face it bravely, with the conviction that it leads to eternal joy. As John Donne has written in his Holy Sonnets:

> Death be not proud, though some have called thee
> Mighty and dreadful, for thou art not so,
> For, those whom thou think'st thou dost overthrow
> Die not, poor death, nor yet canst thou kill me.

Or, as the Hindu poet, Rabindranath Tagore has written more gently:

Death is not extinguishing the light.
It is putting out the lamp because the dawn has come.

SR. CLARICE FISCHETTE 2-24-2003

Readings: Is. 12-2-6
1 Cor. 13: 8-13
Jn. 15: 1-11

Saturday afternoon, as I was preparing some reflections for Sr. Clarice's funeral, I went to the internet and searched for "You are My Sunshine." I found a server engine that not only gave me the words, but played the melody as well. So there I was, sitting at my desk, with this song filling the room; and I'm half-expecting to hear a cheery voice asking: "Would you like some ice today?"

One of the things I learned on the internet is that "You are My Sunshine" is the state song of Louisiana. A helpful bit of information for trivial pursuits, perhaps. But be that as it may be, we know that "You are My Sunshine" was the theme song that identified Sr. Clarice. As she sped through the halls of the Motherhouse with her ice cart, she not only sang her song, she embodied it. She was a breath of sunshine and cheeriness – with a beautiful simplicity and a wondrous sense of unself-conscious joy.

As I think of her and her life among us the word that keeps coming back to me is JOY. And the term I use is "unself-conscious joy." By that I mean; it was spontaneous in her. She didn't have to think about it, then do it. No, her life was centered in giving joy. She didn't think much about receiving joy. She found her joy in sharing joy, in giving joy to others.

If joy identified her life on earth, it surely defines her life in heaven. Death is the sacrament of joy. For it is the experience of total absorption into God. We become fully in God what we have been striving to become all through our lives. We become fully who we are; and we become it in joy.

As I was thinking about this, I decided to see what St Thomas Aquinas had to say about joy. Now I don't suppose there are many of you who are regular readers of St. Thomas. In fact, off-hand, the only one I can think of who might fit in that category is Msgr. Emmett Murphy. But even he would have to admit that reading the *Summa Theologiae* is not something you would have on your short list of exciting reading.

But I must say I was surprised when I read what he has to say about *gaudium*, joy. He is speaking about the joy of the blessed in heaven. His language becomes quite ecstatic. In fact, he gets so roused up in writing about the joy of heaven that he pulls out all the stops. He even goes so far as to invent a new Latin word. Thus, he says that the blessed in heaven are "perfectly full of joy" (he uses the Latin words *perfecte plenum*), which means "perfectly full." Everything that the blessed ever desired is fulfilled when they enter into God.

But Aquinas is not satisfied with this statement. For, he insists, the blessed in heaven obtain more joy than they could possibly have dreamed of. To say this he has to coin a new Latin word: *superplenum*, superfull. What he is trying to say is that their joy is not just the regular grade of joy. It's premium joy. Joy beyond our possibility to conceive.

In proof of this extravagant statement St. Thomas quotes St. Paul's words: "It has not even entered into the human mind what God has prepared for those who love God."

Note how St. Thomas is going Jesus one better. In his discourse at the Last Supper Jesus says to his beloved disciples: Your joy will be complete. Thomas says it will be even more than that. It will be joy full measure, joy flowing over and spreading quite beyond our hopes and expectations.

As we gather this afternoon for this Eucharist to celebrate the earthly life of this woman of joy, we may experience a twinge of sadness, at the thought that death has separated us from her and her from us. But that sense of separation is illusory. The language we so often use about our loved ones who are with God is often bad theology. We speak of them, for instance, as "our beloved dead." This is indeed poor theology. Sure, it is true that Clarice died, but *she is not dead.* Don't we say in the preface of the Mass:

"Vita mutatur, not tollitur. ("Life is changed, it is not taken away."). Death is not life's end; it is the beginning of true life: the life for which we were all made, a life of perfect union with God, life immortal.

Another term we use that also expresses a bad theology is the term "the faithful departed." Those who have gone through the portals of death to full life in God have not left us. Karl Rahner has written:

I have often reflected upon the surest comfort for those who mourn. It is this: a firm faith in the real and continual presence of our loved ones to us; it is the clear and penetrating conviction that death has not destroyed them, nor carried them away. They are not even absent, but living near us, transfigured, having lost, in their glorious change, no delicacy of their souls, no tenderness of their hearts, nor a special preference in their affection...Those who on earth were ordinary Christians become perfect... those who were good become sublime....

We do not see them, but they see us. Though invisible to us, they are not absent."

We need to keep in our memory that our loved ones who have died do not go someplace; they go to Someone: they go to God. Just take a second to reflect on what that means in terms of what we understand about God. The great mystery about God – a mystery that is at the heart of all spirituality -- is the "Everywhereness" of God. But if God is everywhere and our loved ones go to God, then they are where God is. Surely this is a great and wondrous mystery. But it is the reason why Rahner can say: We do not see them, but they see us. They are invisible to us, but not absent.

Sr. Clarice has entered into the fullness of joy, indeed, into its super-fullness. As we remember her today,

- 164 -

we do so with the confident hope that a bit of that super-fullness will overflow into us. She will teach us how to share in that joy that surpasses even the deepest and most prayerful yearnings of our hearts. She will help to open our minds and hearts in order that we, like she, may be "surprised by joy."

SR. HELEN LOUISE KIRBY 2-2-2002

Readings: Malachi 3:1-4
Heb. 2: 14-18
Lk. 2: 22-40

Today's wonderful feast is about a family – a holy family – who go to the temple in Jerusalem to fulfill the prescriptions of the law of Moses. This feast is also about two elderly people: a man and a woman. We are not told much about Simeon's life before this event, nor about Anna's life. I picture them as wonderful persons who, "when there was question of many things to be done in the community and the choice was left to them, chose what was more lowly and difficult and left to others what was easier and brought more honor." (Maxim 47) Actually, all we are told about them is that they were *waiting* for the Lord's Messiah. The verb used for "waiting" (*prosdexomenos*) means "waiting with eagerness," "waiting with expectancy." It means "a readiness to receive to one's self." The picture the word evokes is a person with open arms looking forward to embrace someone. And of course that is exactly what happened, as Simeon and Anna embrace the Child whose coming they had so longingly awaited.

It doesn't take a great leap of imagination to transport this scene to Sr. Helen Louise's room in the Infirmary this past week. I remember saying to her last Sunday: "Helen, God is waiting for you." With a little touch of impatience, she said: "Well, I'm waiting for God." As if to say: "What is God waiting for? I am ready, eager to embrace God."

And that is precisely what she did on Thursday. She embraced God by embracing death. All Helen's life was a preparation, a waiting if you will, for that exquisite moment when in the act of death she would embrace her God and Savior. I say "the act of death," for death is not a passion (namely, something that we endure). It is an action that we perform. At the deepest level of being – below the level of consciousness – a dying person says: "Yes" to God. This moment which is beyond our vision, beyond our power to see, is the culminating moment of a person's life. It was the culminating moment in the life of Sr. Helen Louise, as she opened her being to embrace God or rather to be embraced by God. What joy she must have experienced in the Lord's coming!

Someone has said: "Life is what we do while we are waiting to die." There is something worth reflecting on in this seemingly puzzling statement. It doesn't mean that the very wonderful things Helen Louise did in so many different and difficult ministries during the days of her mortal existence were unimportant, only that they were not ultimate.

That is why no matter what it is we are doing in life, it is, in ultimate terms, always in a context of waiting. Waiting for the greatest and most important act we shall ever perform. That most important and ultimate act for each of us and all of us, as it was for Sr. Helen Louise, is the act of death, the act in which we make our final life-choice. The act in which we embrace God and are embraced by God. The celebration of Sr. Helen Louise's death helps us to appreciate ever more fully that most exquisite prayer that we say each day at Mass: "Free us from all anxiety, as we wait in joyful hope for the coming of our Savior, Jesus Christ."

One day last week, when I saw Sister, she asked me if in heaven she would see her parents and also little Kirby and all her relatives and friends. I said: "Helen, I am sure you will." I felt quite assured in saying this to her. After all, St. Thomas Aquinas said as much. So I am in safe company. Yet I have to say that I am not sure exactly what it means.

The difficulty we face in talking about heaven is that we are talking about something we have not yet experienced. People tend to think of heaven in terms of their own desires. Thus a medieval generation, in which people worked from sunup to sundown, easily saw heaven as a place of eternal rest. We have inherited some of that mentality. We do say: "*Requiescat in pace.*" (May he [she] rest in peace.") And there are times when a good rest can be very appealing to us.

Yet the fact is that we live in an age that stresses growth and maturing. We tend, therefore, to see heaven more in terms of a dynamic entering into the fullness of our own potential as human beings and as followers of Jesus. We become fully ourselves: something we have tried to do all through life without ever fully succeeding. So it makes sense to talk about heaven in terms of growth, ever deepening knowledge of God, deepening of friendships, growing in knowledge and love of one another. This certainly must mean seeing and getting to know more and more fully our relatives and friends. Maybe even those who weren't friends. So, yes, Helen, you will see your loved ones.

Indeed, it can be safely said that in heaven we will be perfect and yet perfectible. We will continue the joy of growing in knowledge and love. At the same time we shall be at rest. For we shall have overcome what we never seem able to overcome in this life: the restlessness that so clearly describes the human condition. That restlessness is really the expression of our expectant waiting, our longing for what only heaven can give. As Augustine put it: "You have made us for Yourself, O Lord, and our hearts are restless until they find their rest in You."

And so, Sr. Helen Louise, when I saw you at the Infirmary last Monday, you had lost consciousness and we expected you would go to God then. So I say to you now what I said then: "Good bye, Helen. I'll see you in heaven."

SR. MADELEINE LOUISE HEALY 3-15-2001

Readings: 1 Cor. 2: 7-13
Jn. 20: 11-18

The picture of Sr. Madeleine Louise that I shall always remember is that of her sitting in the eighth pew of this chapel leading our music. Her eyesight had become so bad that she could not read the music without help. So there she sat with the music in one hand and the magnifying glass in the other hand.

She used to knock regularly on my door and come in to give me a report on her eyes. Always she wanted prayers and I promised them to her. In fact, more than a year ago, when she came to tell me the latest about her eye problems, I said to her: "From now on each day I am going to say the Magnificat at evening prayer for your intentions and specifically I will pray that your eyesight will be improved." On Monday morning that prayer was answered in the best possible way. For on Monday her eyesight was not just improved. It was completely restored. Indeed it was more than restored. It was transformed. The first antiphon for morning prayer on Monday cried out: "I thirst for God, the living stream. When will I see God's face?" It was a prayer Madeleine didn't have to say. By the time we came to put that question in prayer at Monday morning prayer, she already had the answer to it. She has that perfect vision which we call the beatific vision. She has seen the face of God.

Not only does death enable her to see the face of God. It also makes it possible for her to see her own face. Did you ever stop to think that you cannot see your own face? And your eyes —which are sometimes called the windows of the soul —you can't see them either. You see with your eyes. But you cannot see your eyes. You might want to say: But I can see my face and I can see my eyes, when I look into a mirror. Ah, but it is not your eyes that you see in the mirror, but the reflection of them. It is not your face that you see in the mirror, but the reflection of your face. The reflection of your face is not your face.

This inability to see our own face is a kind of metaphor that tells us that we do not really know ourselves. Our face is the most expressive part of our physical being: it registers our thoughts, our feeling, our emotions. It is our face that makes us vividly present to others. It is something seen that tells us about what is unseen, something visible that tells us of something invisible. Suppose you were to walk into a room and see 20 people – each without a face.

To put it mildly it would be an eerie, unsettling experience. You would be seeing a group of "nobodies." To think of a person without a face is to imagine someone with no personal identity.

A person's face then is a symbol of that person's identity. Therefore when I say that we cannot see our own faces, I am really saying that we cannot know our own identity. We cannot know what makes us unique.

We can talk about the many qualities and gifts of character that so beautifully emerged in Sr. Madeleine Louise's life among us. Yet I dare say that there is no one who is able to describe Sr. Madeleine's personal uniqueness. Vladimir Lossky is his book *The Mystical Theology of the Eastern Church* has written what I think is a very perceptive insight about the limitations of every attempt to describe an individual person. He says: "When we wish to define or characterize a person, we gather together certain traits of character, but these are never uniquely personal, because they are characteristics that are [also] possessed [in varying degrees] by other persons." "There is," he says, "nothing in nature which properly describes what is proper to this person and this person only. For what is proper to each person, what makes each person who she is, is always unrepeatable." Hence, try as we will, we cannot capture in our words that which makes a person the unique reality that she is. We cannot capture in words the uniqueness that for her 89 years on earth we called Sr. Madeleine Louise.

Not only can we not define her uniqueness. She herself, while in our midst, could not herself put words on that uniqueness. It remained a mystery to her, perhaps even more of a mystery to her than it was to us. It was a mystery known only to God. To put this into metaphorical language, she could not see her own face. Only God could see her face.

The wonderful thing about the experience of death is that death is the uncovering of that mystery. All through our mortal life we struggle with the question: "Who am I?" At various times we get certain insights into the answer, but never do we capture the answer in its fullness. Our whole life story is our effort to affirm the unique person we really are. It is our vain effort to see our own face. But never in this mortal life are we able to see our own face. Never are we able to make a full affirmation of that which makes us uniquely who we are.

But the wonderful thing about us is that every person has the opportunity to make this affirmation and to make it in a final and definitive way, not *before* death, not *after* death, but *in* death: that is, at the moment of death. All through the mortal phase of our existence before death, we say "Yes" to God and "Yes" to our unique self, but it is always a "Yes" that is partial and incomplete. At the moment of death the human person is set free from all the limitations that in this mortal life cloud our decisions and prevent us from making the choice we want to make, but as yet cannot.

To put it another way, death is the final and decisive sacrament of our encounter with the Risen Jesus, as He strives to make us into himself. It is only in the sacrament of death that Jesus' task of remaking us is fully complete, as we surrender our total being to his transforming touch. Death is thus the sacrament of total absorption into God; yet it is an experience that is uniquely personal to each one of us. We become fully in God what we have been striving to become all our lives (even if we didn't know that that was what we were striving for). We become in God the totally unique person that each one of us is. It is a uniqueness that is unrepeatable in any other person. This is one way of understanding Jesus' words in the Gospel: "In my Father's house there are many dwelling places." In death I get to know at last the "I" that heretofore was known only to God. I at last awaken to who I really am. In death I get to see my own face.

Thus death was the greatest experience in Sr. Madeleine's life. What a joy to realize that she has achieved the goal of every human existence. Now at last she sees the face of God. But also she knows fully and joyfully the unique person she is, for she experiences that uniqueness where alone it can be found: namely, in God. Yes, in God she sees her own face!

SR. MARY MATTHEW FENNESSY 1-19-2001

Readings: Is. 12: 2-6
Rom. 8:31-34, 38-39
Jn. 17: 24-26

Sr. Jane Joseph told me a delightful story the other day. It was about St. Monica's convent in the days when Msgr. Bergen was pastor. Sr. Louise Marie had just been appointed as principal of the school. Just before school opened she was called to the convent parlor, where she found a charming young woman, beautifully dressed. The young woman told Sister that she would like to apply for the position of French teacher.   Sister was delighted, assured the young woman that she would like to hire her, but first she would have to talk with Msgr. Bergen.   Sr. Louise Marie then returned to the community room and told the Sisters about this lovely young lady who had applied for the position of French teacher and how pleased she was with her.   Finally, some of the Sisters who knew what was going on told her that the charming young lady was already on the faculty. In fact, she was already a Sister of St. Joseph. The charming young lady was Sr. Mary Matthew *incognita* - in secular dress.

Now there's a great story; and it's about a lady with a great sense of humor.

Many years ago – back in the '40s when I was ordained – a story such as this would have been disconcertingly out of place at a funeral liturgy.   Funerals in those days were not happy events. Black vestments were worn. A black cloth was placed over the casket. The mournful tones of the *Dies Irae* were sung.   The readings were generally about judgment. The homily was a plea for prayers for the person who had died and a warning to the rest of us to be ready for the time of reckoning that would sooner or later come for all of us. It was a liturgy in which joy lost out to mourning, in which hope struggled with fear – fear for the eternal salvation of someone dear to us. And not infrequently, fear was stronger than hope.

What a difference in funeral liturgies today. You heard the three readings of this liturgy. Sr. Mary Matthew chose them herself.   And in them you can see something of the kind of happy spirit that described her, the same spirit that emerges in the delightful story of her pretended job quest.

Notice that the readings she chose set the tone for the liturgy. The reading from Isaiah is an expression of confident joy. Isaiah's words become the words of Sr. Mary Matthew. "God is my savior. I am confident and unafraid. All my life I have experienced joy. I have drunk at the fountains of salvation. So I ask you, my friends: give thanks to the Lord. Sing God's praises, for God has done wondrous things for me."

The text from the Epistle to the Romans is another expression of sheer confidence. In Christ she is united with God and nothing can break the ties of that unity. Life can't do it. Death can't do it. Angels can't do it. Nothing can separate me, she tells us, from the love of God that comes to us in Christ Jesus our Lord. What a stirring expression of hope and joy and peace.

In her choice of the Gospel reading, Sr. Mary Matthew shows such faith in God's love that she confidently inserts herself into Jesus' prayer to the Father as one of those given to Jesus by the Father and one to whom Jesus has revealed the Father and called into the oneness of the very life of God.

We can rejoice with Sr. Mary Matthew, as she goes to God with confidence and love and joy. Despite the regrettable "things" happening in the Church these days, we should be grateful that we live at a time when Christians recognize the reality of sin, but are not overwhelmed by it. We, pre-baby-boomers, can remember the days when the thought of sin seemed to dominate our spiritual lives. It was a time when we felt that we lived the life of grace only precariously. We almost took it for granted that after a certain amount of time had elapsed, we surely must have fallen out of grace into the state of sin. We were often uneasy till we got into the anonymity of the confessional and received absolution. Especially for the spiritually sensitive, those were not happy days.

But those days have passed. In our day we have come to realize that *GRACE IS MORE ORIGINAL THAN SIN.* For those who strive to live their Christian faith, the normal state is the state of grace, not the state of sin. For those who strive to live their faith, death is a wonderful beginning of a new life of full communion with God. As I say this, I am happy to let you know that Pope John Paul II agrees with me. In one of his weekly audiences he talked about heaven. In this context he spoke about the mercy of God. "Those who accept God in their lives and are sincerely open to God's love enjoy at the moment of death that fullness of communion with God which is the goal of human existence." Heaven, he goes on to say, is "neither an abstraction nor a physical place in the clouds, but a living and personal relationship of union with the Holy Trinity. It is our definitive meeting with God." (July 21,1999). The Pope is telling us that heaven is the goal for which we were made. It is joy without alloy.

Those of us who are alarmed at the efforts being made, often in high places, to reinterpret the Second Vatican Council, can take heart from the significant changes that have occurred in the funeral liturgy. These are changes that cannot be reversed. They are signs of life in the Church. They bring joy into an experience that once was most often mournful. The fact that Sr. Mary Matthew chose her own readings, the heart-felt confidence and joy that those readings embody are proof to us that, whatever side roads we may get lost in at times, we are moving in the right direction. We are listening to the Spirit who will lead us where we must go. We can approach life with a light-heartedness similar to that of a young woman in a convent parlor looking, so it seemed, for a position teaching French. Sr. Mary Matthew's entrance into the heavenly parlor was just as much fun and so much more, but there she had no need, nor even the possibility, of going *incognita.*

SISTER JOAN OF ARC PERO 8-16-2000

Readings: 1 Cor. 2:7-10
Rev. 21: 1-5, 6-7
Jn. 14:1-6

There is perhaps no area of human existence in which Christian Faith is more counter-cultural than the area of human existence that we are here to celebrate this evening. We are here to celebrate the death of Sr. Joan of Arc. Our culture has one way of looking at what we celebrate tonight. *The American Heritage Dictionary*, which is a part of that culture, defines the noun "death" as the "termination of life." And the verb "to die" it describes as "to stop living." The card announcing Sr. Joan of Arc's death offers a very different view of death. The statement on that announcement card is a strong counter-cultural statement: "Sr. Joan of Arc entered into eternal life." It would be hard to find a stronger contrast than that between these two statements about death: death as the "termination of life" and "death as entrance into eternal life."

The way people look at death determines, or at least contributes to, the way they live before death. The one truly worthwhile question that everyone has to face is this question: "Does death *terminate everything* or does death *begin something* -- something far greater than we have ever known or can ever know in this life?"

We have made our choice: we accept our answer to that question. We believe that death begins something new and wonderful. We believe this not because we have experienced it, but because we have the certainty of faith. For Sr. Joan of Arc it is no longer a matter of faith. She knows with the certainty of experience: the new and glorious experience which was God's early birthday present to her. Her birthday was just a few days away. But divine Largesse said: "Why wait?" And so she entered last Saturday into eternal life.

One thing troubles me tonight. When we go to the Missal to find prayers for Sr. Joan of Arc, we have to go to a section called Masses for the Dead, I find that troubling because I cannot think of her as dead. She is alive – alive in a much fuller sense than you and I are alive.

When God created Sr. Joan of Arc, God gave her an eternal existence. Part of that existence was mortal: the life she lived on earth. That part of her life ended with her death on August 9th. But the death that ended her mortal existence ushered in the beginning of the immortal phase of her existence: her life with God.

Thus, human existence is *eternal*, but in two stages. On the full trajectory of human existence, death is just a "blip," so to speak, between mortality and immortality. Why should we allow that blip, that moment, death, to determine the language we use to describe those who have passed into new life? So, instead of praying for Sr. Joan of Arc as dead, I want to pray for her as alive and immortal in that wondrous company that we call the communion of saints. In fact, I want to pray not just for her but to her and especially with her.

So we come together tonight to celebrate life, not death.

First, we want to celebrate her life with us during her earthly sojourn. All hundred years of them! So many people here have so many glorious memories of this wonderful lady! We celebrate her vivacity, her wonderful sense of humor, her beautiful smile, her penchant for losing her rosary in the wash, her clarity of mind right to the very end, as she insisted: "I've got all my buttons."

We want also tonight to celebrate that side of her life that we cannot know, that side that is mystery, that side which we can only try to imagine: the glorious new life that is hers in her return to the God from whom she came. This is what Paul is describing when he tells us that it is "what no eye has seen, nor ear heard, nor the human mind conceived: what God has prepared for those who love God." (1 Cor., 2:9)

But we come also tonight for ourselves: to face the reality of our own deaths. We are here, because her death helps us to see that death --which is darkness for so many people -- is for us a wondrous light. For we view death through the eyes of faith. It is this faith-picture that is evoked for us in the book of *Revelation*: no more tears, no more mourning or crying out, no more pain. Everything made new!

In the Gospel Jesus tells us that he wants us to be where he is. In a sense we are where he is, because as the Risen One Jesus is always at our side. Yet in our mortal life, we never have that total awareness that the Risen Jesus is really there. We rejoice tonight that Sr. Joan of Arc is now enjoying this totality of awareness. She had to wait a long time for that wondrous moment of ecstatic joy. None of us knows how long we shall have to wait.

But, as we give her back to God, we must not be afraid to wait, with a kind of quiet joy, for this wondrous moment that one day will be ours. And there must be no fear or anxiety in the waiting. In what is surely one of its most beautiful prayers – and a prayer that is about as counter-cultural as you can get -- the Eucharistic liturgy teaches us to pray each day: "Protect us from all anxiety, as we wait in joyful hope for the coming of our Saviour, Jesus Christ."

SR. NATHALIE BRAHLER – 10-29-1999

Is. 26: 6-7, 9
Philippians 3: 20-21
Jn. 1: 44-51

What are we to say about a Sister whose life was two months short of spanning the entire 20th century? Who lived through 18 presidencies of the United States? Who served the Church under nine popes going back to Leo XIII, under all the bishops of Rochester from Bishop McQuaid on, under all the superior generals or presidents of the congregation of the Sisters of St. Joseph with the exception of Mother Stanislaus? In case you never noticed, I am no youngster myself, yet Sr. Nathalie entered the congregation of the Sisters of St. Joseph the year I was born. What indeed are we to say? Certainly not: why did God take her at so tender an age? No, what we celebrate tonight is not the quantity of years (in which she certainly outshines all of us), but the quality of a magnificent life dedicated to God, to her sisters, and to all those she served through the many decades of her wholesome life.

Who was Sr. Nathalie? The Gospel, which speaks of her patron saint, perhaps says something of the kind of person she was. Philip introduces his friend Nathaniel to Jesus. Jesus looks at Nathaniel and knows immediately that here is someone very special: someone straightforward, honest, gentle, with never any deceit in his heart. Jesus looks at him and says: "Here is an Israelite in whom there is no deceit." The Revised English Bible conveys more clearly what Jesus meant to say. It puts it this way: "Here is an Israelite worthy of the name; there is nothing false in him."

In speaking of Sr. Nathalie, I want to paraphrase Jesus' words about her patron saint and say of her: "Here is a Christian worthy of the name. Here is a Sister of St. Joseph worthy of the name. There is nothing false in her."

"There is nothing false in her." With the certainty of faith I can say that of Sr. Nathalie now. I don't think I can say it of myself or even of anyone else here in this chapel. For I am quite convinced that Thomas Merton is right when he says that every one of us is shadowed by a false self, an illusory person. My false self is a self that tried to manipulate others or even allow itself to be manipulated by others. It is the self that seeks approval and adulation at all costs. It wants everything to center around itself. It's a brittle self – that is easily hurt, a self that cannot brook criticism or disagreement. The more such a false self is in control of my life, the more miserable life becomes. As

Thomas Merton writes: "The only true joy on earth is to escape from the prison of our own false self and enter by love into union with the God of life who dwells in the heart of each one of us."

This is what Christian spirituality is all about: escaping from the false self (and we have to realize that it is there before we can escape from it). Escaping from our false self enables us to discover our true self which is hidden in God. The process of this escape is a long process. It takes a lifetime. It is a movement into the mystery of our true self which is tied up with the mystery of God. For that is where our true self is: in God. There are, I am sure, times in the lives of each of us when we experience glimmerings of a mystery in life that we know is there, yet cannot explain. There are times when we touch God – if only for a moment. In that moment, for that moment, we are truly ourselves. We are, as it were, in another world. A world in which there is no falsity, no illusion, only truth and reality and goodness and love. This is the world of the mystery of God, of the mystery of our true selves.

Yet when we distinguish this world and that other world, we must be careful not to think that we are talking about geography. That "other" world, which alone is fully real, does not exist apart from this world, say like another planet might exist in our solar system apart from planet earth. No, that other world commingles with this world. We can discover it, if only partially, in this life.

Death is the full discovery of that other world. It was always there, but we didn't know it. For that other world is not a place. It is the life of God communicated to us: partially in this life, fully in death. Life is a journey in which we seek to reach that other world. The paradox is that we are already in that world. But we have to discover that we are there. Our prayers, our deeds, our loves, our joys and sorrows, our failures and frustrations are all ways in which we are led to make that discovery. Death is the final step in that discovery. Thus death is not going somewhere. It is finding Someone, Someone who was always there, but never quite fully recognized. For we die into God. We find ourselves, our true selves, in God.

Those 102 years of searching and journeying are over for Sr. Nathalie. She has achieved life's purpose. She experiences fully the joy of life in God's presence. As we reflect on this joy that is hers, it is a saving experience for us to realize that we live every moment of our lives in that same divine presence. The sad thing is that we are so accustomed to live at a surface level of consciousness that so easily precludes contact with the deepest realities of life. We need to treasure those precious moments that come to us when we know that we are in touch with a mystery in life that we know is there, yet cannot explain. And I am not speaking necessarily or even especially about "churchy" moments, but moments of every day life. Our God is a God of surprises who refuses to be held captive. We cannot lock God up in a church building or any other building or place. God is where people are. God acts where people are.

The more we open ourselves to the mystery of God in our lives, the more we are able to divest ourselves of what is false and phony and illusory in us. We move ever closer to becoming our true selves, to becoming like Nathaniel and Sr. Nathalie: persons in whom there is no deceit, nothing false.

SR. FRANCIS GERARD SMALT 9-9-1999

Readings:1 Cor. 2: 7-10
Jn. 11: 5-27

Probably not too many know that Sr. Francis Gerard and I were singing partners. Well, sort of. When I first came to the motherhouse in 1980 (or rather returned, since I had been here earlier), there was a 4:00 p.m. anticipated Sunday Mass on Saturday. It was a rather slim congregation – about ten people scattered to the ten corners of the chapel. But Sr. Francis Gerard was in the front pew. And she led the music and I joined in. There may have been a few other voices chiming in. But she and I were really the backbone of that 4:00 choir. We had a kind of special cacaphonous harmony: we were especially good at doing quivering quilismas. And our episemas were out of this world. Of course we hardly ever started on the same key. That didn't really matter. For what we did together had a kind of beauty of its own – a kind of weird beauty. And I have a feeling that God looked upon what God heard and said it was very good. God is tone-deaf when it comes to people who are trying to do their best.

When I used to go the St. Joseph's Convent on Sunday for Mass, it was always a joy to be greeted by Sr. Francis Gerard, and almost every Sunday I was there she managed to greet me with her warm smile and happy grin. She was, is, a wonderful lady. And she has gone to God. Or, as I like to put it, she died into God. And, as I say this, I am happy to point out that Pope John Paul II agrees with me! At a general audience, given this past July, he raised a few eyebrows when he said that heaven "is not an abstraction or a physical place among the clouds, but a living and personal relationship with the Holy Trinity." He was speaking about the mercy of God. "Those who accept God in their lives and are sincerely open to God's love at the moment of death enjoy that fullness of communion with God which is the goal of human existence." (*Tablet,* July 31, 1999)

And that fullness of communion with God is communion of the whole person. Sr. Francis Gerard died into God without sight, without hearing. Now she is full of seeing, full of hearing, full of beauty. How much she must now appreciate those words of Paul: "Eye has not seen, ear has not heard, nor has it so much dawned on people what God has prepared for those who love God." (1Cor.:2:7-10)

When we speak of a person's death, we often say: She (he) has fallen asleep. Notice how these are the words

Jesus uses to describe the death of his friend Lazarus. "Our beloved Lazarus," he tells his disciples, "has fallen asleep." The disciples, realizing that sleep can be restorative of life, say: "Lord, if he is asleep, his life will be saved." Then Jesus tells them plainly: "Lazarus is dead…Let us go to him." Then followed that wonderful event of the raising of Lazarus.

Why do we describe death as falling asleep? It is because death is so similar to sleep. When we fall asleep, we lose consciousness to reawake the next day to the same conscious mortal life that we briefly let go of the night before. When we die, we lose consciousness and awake to a super-conscious immortal existence. Shakespeare has a wonderful description of sleep in the words of Lady Macbeth who cannot sleep, as she remembers the terrible deed of the king's murder.

Sleep that knits up the raveled sleeve of care,
The death of each day's life,
Balm of hurt minds, chief nourisher in life's feast.

Some people work too hard and deprive themselves of sleep. But they can't do it indefinitely. Sleep is a biological necessity, but it's also an act of faith. Sleep is disengaging ourselves from the often confused realities of daily life, as we sink trustingly into the arms of a loving and caring God. Sleep prays: "Into your hands, O Lord, I commend my spirit." Sleep is letting go. It's complete surrender to God.

Charles Peguy in his *Basic Verities* has a wonderful poem about sleep. God speaks and says:
Sleep is people's friend.
Sleep is the friend of God.
Sleep is perhaps the most beautiful thing I have created…

But they tell me there are people
Who work well and sleep badly.
What a lack of confidence in me.
I pity them. I have it against them. A little. They
don't trust me.
Like the child who innocently lies in its mother's
arms,
Thus they do not lie
Innocently in the hands of my Providence...
Poor people, they don't know what is good.
They look after their business very well during the
day.
But they haven't enough confidence in me to let me
look after it during the night.
As if I wasn't capable of looking after it one night.
Those who don't sleep are unfaithful to hope
And it's the greatest infidelity.

Sleep, therefore, is our rehearsal for death. It's a practice run, if you will. We have to learn to do it well. We conclude night prayer in the liturgical office with a twofold petition: "Give us a restful night and a peaceful death." So far for us, God has granted the first petition: giving us, as God does, a restful night. For each of us the day will come, as it came for Sr. Francis Gerard on Monday, when God will grant both petitions: a restful night and a peaceful death.

Death is complete and total surrender to God. Sleep -- that daily handing over of our lives to God that we do each night --helps prepare us to make that final surrender. The love of God works *with* us during the day, but *for* us during the night. Death, that final sleep, when it comes, ushers us, not into some place in the heavens, but into Love's habitat, that is, into God.

For us who believe in the Risen Jesus, death has lost all its sting. With his resurrection, death died. So, tonight we can rejoice with Sr. Francis Gerard who now dwells in God who is Love. We can stare death in the face and address it with the words of John Donne:

> Death, be not proud, though some have called thee
> Mighty and dreadful, for thou art not so.
> For, those, whom thou thinkest thou dost overthrow,
> Die not, poor death, nor yet canst thou kill me.

As we move toward today's shadows into night, let us pray hopefully and confidently: "God, grant us a restful night and a peaceful death. And may Sr. Francis Gerard rest in peace. Amen."

SR. MARIE THERESE WARTH 6-28-1996

Readings: 1 Peter 4: 8-11A
No second reading
John 12: 23-28

Sr. Marie Therese, this is the second homily I prepared for this liturgy in which we are giving you back to God unto God's glory and your eternal happiness. I had already prepared one. Then I found out you had chosen your own readings and they were completely different readings from the ones I had picked. So I had to start over again. At one point I thought: maybe I could give both homilies and let you take your pick. An alternative I quickly rejected as too great a strain on this congregation (not on you).

When I learned what the readings were that you chose, the first question that came to my mind was: why did you choose them? Don't misunderstand. I am not suggesting that they are not good readings. They certainly are. They're strong and demanding. I just wondered what you had in mind when you picked them.

The Gospel reading is a masterpiece of Johannine theology: it stresses the glory that God will bestow on Jesus if he perseveres and does not seek release from the cross that shadows him. Jesus speaks about his hour: a very prominent term in the Fourth Gospel. His hour is the hour of his glorification, of his return to God, but it will be achieved only through his dying. He must die, as the grain of wheat, put in the earth, must die. If a grain of wheat is just put into the ground but just remains there as a grain of wheat, it will not produce fruit. To produce fruit it has to cease to be itself and become something greater, namely, the fruit. When you chose that Gospel, was there a bit of autobiography in the choice? Were you perhaps thinking of the hour that someday was coming for you, when you would have to die fully to yourself so as to become something greater; that you would have to die in order to enter into God's glory? Were you perhaps afraid that when your hour came that you might be moved to say: "Save me from this hour?" Did you choose this reading because you were sure that you wanted to say with Jesus: "No, I don't want to be spared this hour. It was for this reason that I came to this hour?" Did you want to say, again with Jesus, "Father glorify your name?"

And when you chose that Gospel about "glorifying God," did you have any thought, I wonder, that your Mass of Christian burial would take place on the feast of St. Irenaeus, who spoke so splendidly about glory? He wrote: "The glory of God is a human being fully alive?" the term "glory" is used in the Bible to describe manifestations of God. And to Irenaeus the human being is in a most special sense such a manifestation. That is precisely what has happened to you. You have died with Christ and entered with him into the glory of God. And we can only praise God and marvel at the insight that chose this reading.

And why, Sister, did you choose that first reading? Most people don't pay much attention to the two letters ascribed to Peter. Paul's are so much better known. I wonder, Sister, was this reading a gift you intended to give to the congregation to which you have given 71 years of your life? Were you offering those who would continue the task of this congregation a kind of mission statement that could guide the future?

If I take that to be your intent, then your mission statement highlights four points, four principles of guidance. The first is this: "Above all, maintain constant love for one another." Every word is important. "Above all" indicates that this is the first and most fundamental principle that must guide community. "Love one another": the word used for love is that very demanding Greek word *agape*. It means a love that is not self-seeking, but other-directed. "Love one another" covers everybody. Whatever our feelings may be at certain times, our love can exclude no one. It's inclusive love or it's not the real thing. This love is described as a love that must be "constant," which means that an occasional reaching out to others is not enough. "Constant" means at all times. This kind of love — for everyone and at all times and unselfishly — requires maintenance. We have to keep working at it. So we are told: "Maintain constant love."

This, then, is the first principle: "Above all, —
maintain —constant — love — for one another."

The second principle is: "Be hospitable to everyone
without complaining." "Hospitable" is a word dripping
with all sorts of implications that are not readily evident
until we analyze the word. It is the Greek word *philoxenoi*.
philos means "friend"; *xenos* means "stranger." The term
"stranger" covers a lot more than we might even want to
consider. The poor, the homeless, the exploited, the
powerless in our society, the abused children and abused
women, people with AIDS, victims of sexual abuse,
pregnant teenagers: all these and many others come under
the rubric of stranger. *Phioxenoi,* therefore, — this being
friend to strangers — is no easy burden. It helps us realize
what Jesus meant when he said: "What you do to the least
of my sisters and brothers, you do to me." And just so we
don't try to get ourselves off the hook, we are told how we
are to befriend the stranger: "without complaining."

The third principle is to be good stewards —
stewards of the gifts God has given to each one of us. We
are good stewards when we use our gifts, not for our own
advantage, but for the good of all. And we can do it
because we have the strength that God supplies.

The fourth principle gives us the ultimate reason for
the other three: namely, we do all this so that God may be
glorified in all things. There it is again: glory. We come
back to that goal that was expressed in the Gospel: the
glory of God. And also we can hear ringing in our ears the
words of Irenaeus: "The glory of God is the human person
fully alive."

So, let us sum up this gift of a mission statement
that Sr. Marie Therese has offered us in her choice of this
reading:

(1) Maintain constant love for one another. (2) Be friends to strangers, especially those who need your friendship most. (3) Be good stewards of the charisms and gifts that come from God and come with the strength to use them; and (4) do all this for the glory of God.

Sr. Mary Ida told me that Sr. Marie Therese carried on a wide correspondence --keeping in touch with friends, relatives, former pupils. Just imagine what her correspondence would have been, if she had had e-mail. But now, in the glory of God, she is on the heavenly internet and can get messages out to anyone. For the heavenly Internet is but a very modern metaphor we can give to a very ancient reality that has always been with us, namely, the communion of saints, and the connection we have with all the saints that makes us one with them. Whether we have computers or not, we are all on that heavenly Internet.

Thank you, Sr. Marie Therese, for the readings you chose for us. May we hear deeply what they say to us. And don't worry about that other homily. I may be able to adapt it a bit and use it one day for one of your friends.

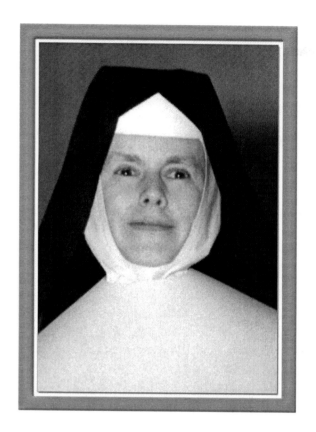

SR. ROSE TERESA CLARK 2-2-1995

Readings: Malachi 3: 104
Hebrew 2:14-18
Luke 2: 22-40

Today is the fortieth day of Christmas: absolutely the last possible day for sending out Christmas cards. True, we have been in what the liturgy calls ordinary time for four weeks now. But it really isn't fully ordinary time, until after we have celebrated the feast of Our Lord's Presentation. Today is, as it were, a kind of last filing for Christmas. Tomorrow we really go into ordinary time. All of us, that is, except Sr. Rose Teresa.

She doesn't go into ordinary time. She doesn't even go into extraordinary time. She takes a might leap out of time. She goes beyond any time into the timelessness of God. On this feast of light she goes into the Light which is God.

When I thought about celebrating her funeral liturgy on the feast of the Presentation, this great feast of light, my imagination went wild for the moment about how we could celebrate her going to God in a most glorious way. I thought of giving everyone in the chapel a lighted candle and then filling the sanctuary with hundreds of burning candles. And yet all this beautiful light would be like darkness compared to the light of God into which she has entered. *Dominus illumination sua.* The Lord God is her light now. She sees everything in and through that Light which is God

Stop to think what this means. Astronauts have gone to the moon; and scientists ambition someday landing people on Mars. But nobody ever speaks of someone going to the sun. For to go to the sun would mean being blinded by the light and consumed by the fire of the sun. Sr. Rose Teresa has gone beyond the sun, beyond Mars, yes, beyond the sun. I don't mean that she has taken a space trip. I mean that she has gone to the Light compared to which the sun is darkness. She has entered into a fire of love compared to which the sun is like a cool, lifeless mass.

It is the very reality of God that will be the light by which she sees. Yes, indeed, she can say with all the fullness of meaning: *Dominus illuminatio mea.* The book of Revelation says in the reading we use for Sunday night compline: "She shall see the Lord face to face and bear God's name on her forehead. The night shall be no more. She will need to light from lamps or the sun, for the Lord God shall give her light and she shall reign forever."

The light that is spoken of in the book of Revelation is not just a light that shows what is outside; it is an inner light too. It illumines the whole person. We go through life, so often not seeing our true inner reality, only half-knowing our true selves. For there are so many false selves all too ready to hide us from the person we truly are. Christian growth is growing in that inner light, whereby we come to know ever more deeply into our own reality.

Enlightenment is a very important term in the language of Christian spirituality. Enlightenment is truly the goal of life. But in this life we never achieve the fullness of that light. There are areas of blunted growth in us, areas of darkness, doubt and uncertainty. Each day we accept the challenge to grow into the light. But somehow the fullness of that inner light manages to elude us.

There is a sign over the Rundel library which says: "The shadows will be behind you if you walk into the light." But more often than we would like to admit, we walk into the shadows instead of into the light.

Death is that breathless experience of seeing ourselves fully and truly as we are. For we see God face to face. We see ourselves in God. Not that God is a kind of mirror that we look into and see what before was partly hidden. No, the vision of God is not just a mirror reflection. It is being in the mirror, so to speak. It is being in God. It is nothing less than being one with God. And that is Sr. Rose Teresa's experience.

The problem we face is that we don't really have the language to say it all, to express the experience that is hers. I say that she is in God. Yet the words are deceptive. It's not as if she goes to some place where God is. Think of it this way. Sr. Rose Teresa in going to God has been filled with the light and consumed by the fire of love that we call

God. Yet the language is still elusive and even illusory. For she is consumed not in the sense of disappearing, but rather in the sense of being embraced. Even that isn't adequate. What I really want to say is that she becomes the sun. Does this mean that I am saying she becomes God? Well, not quite, because I wouldn't want to be accused of heresy. She remains who she is; at the same time, she is fully and truly and totally one with God.

Words flounder. For the reality of this total communion with God that comes with death is so huge that we don't have means, anywhere near adequate, to describe it. We grasp for words. But the wondrous reality of the light and the fire that is God and the entrance into that light and fire that is death so transcend our earthly experience that it is a burden too immense for human words to carry. They break down under the weight of what they can never really describe.

St. Thomas Aquinas never finished his *Summa Theologica*. Why not? It was not that he hadn't the time. It is rather that he had a deep contemplative vision of God. After that he said: "Compared to what I have seen, all that I have written is straw. I can write no more." And his was but a momentary experience of the Light and Love that Sr. Rose Teresa is experiencing forever. She has said her *Nunc dimittis*. With Simeon she can say: "I have seen the salvation you have prepared for your people." But she can also say: "I have not only seen it. I have experienced that salvation. I have experienced the joy and the love and the total happiness which is God's gift of the divine Self." More than enough, surely, for an eternity.

To return to my beginning: that today is the absolutely final day of Christmastime, I want to recall John Milton's beautiful hymn on the morning of Christ's nativity. He calls on the heavenly spheres to testify to the wondrous meaning of this event by moving, in melodious time, in harmony with the symphony of the angels. He has the angelic chorus singing to the accompaniment of the music of the heavenly spheres.

He is of course recalling the Ptolemaic cosmology that believed that the earth was stationary and that the planets revolved around the earth. As they moved about the earth, they touched one another in melodious harmony, a harmony that created what the ancients called the "music of the spheres." It was the belief of ancient culture that Adam and Eve in paradise were able to hear and enjoy "the music of the spheres." That joy and a lot of others, too, were lost with their fall.

Now we know today that Ptolemy's cosmological theory has been discredited by the astronomer Copernicus. The sun really isn't stationary nor do the planets revolve around it as Ptolemy said. But surely that is no reason to say that there is no longer the "music of the spheres." And may we not rightfully ask tonight: is that perhaps one of the special joys of paradise for Sr. Rose Teresa, "hearing and enjoying the music of the spheres"?

SR. MARIE RENE PEGNAM 10-13-1994

Readings: 1 Cor. 2:6-10
Jn. 14: 1-12

It was my good fortune to have visited Sr. Marie Rene her last evening on earth: Monday evening. Her mind was perfectly clear. Yet there was a premonition of something coming. I sensed, as I think she did too, what Emily Dickenson called "death's tremendous nearness."

We talked about it. I asked her if she was afraid. She said: No.Are you ready for the great adventure? She said: Yes. But, before she embarked on the great adventure, there were things that had to be cleared up. She had to know what was happening in the world she was about to leave. Her love for history linked her to that world in its concreteness. She understood well the poet's words:

How much can come
And much can go
And yet abide the world.

Before she left she needed to know what was going on in Haiti and in Iraq. And if there is any kind of heavenly newscast, I'm sure she is listening in with that historian's curiosity which she surely still maintains. Heaven does not eliminate, but rather enhances the qualities that help identify us in this life. Only now she sees history from God's angle. She sees it through the eyes of Christ as it were. She shares his compassion for the world. She sees, as Merton puts it in one of his poems, that "The Lord of history weeps into the fire." Yet his tears are redemptive: they help to wipe out the violence and evil that pervade the history that is in the making in our world. The saints in heaven, united to us in the communion of saints, also involve themselves in that redemptive work. This is true especially of those who loved the world and who, while they were here, were most concerned about its history. And surely Sr. Marie Rene was one of them.

That Monday night I talked to her about the time we first got acquainted. It was 44 years ago --on board a ship, the *Roma*, headed for Europe. It was 1950, the Marian year and we were on pilgrimage to visit the Marian shrines in Europe. The trip was organized by the Queen's Work out of St. Louis. The grandiose title given to the trip was "Beyond All Expectations." And indeed it was: no one could have imagined how impossible the living conditions would be or how bad the food. Nine hundred strong, we boarded a ship whose capacity was 450. We were crowded!

and the ship was slow. It took eleven days to cross the Atlantic going east and fifteen days coming back. We were 21 days in Europe and 25 days on the water. One of the engines died on our journey home, and there were times when we wondered if we would ever see land. again or if we were destined to spend the rest of our lives wandering about on the ocean. At any rate, whatever meaning one gives to the phrase, the trip was indeed "beyond all expectations."

And I wonder if this journey (wherein we waited and waited to get home) might not serve as a metaphor for Marie Rene. Her time of suffering was so protracted that it began to seem like more time lived with it than without it. Thinking of that ocean journey as a metaphor for her reminded me of the poet's words:

The waters chased her as she fled,
Not daring look behind;
A billow whispered in her ear,
"Come home with me, my friend..."

We talked about the "Beyond all Expectations" description of the trip, which hardly lived up to its title. "But," she said to me, "it only cost us $690. Where could you get all that travel (25 days at sea, 21 days on land) for $690 today?" And we agreed they were quality days. There were wonderful people on the trip.

We had a lot of fun. In the amateur show held one evening, the Rochester priests (there were about ten of us on the trip) won first prize for a play entitled "Great Expectations." That was my first and only venture as a playwright.

But as we chatted about that trip (and it seemed to brighten her up to speak about it), I think we both knew that a far better journey was about to be hers, as, with "life's departing tide," Christ was coming soon to "claim his living bride." The waters of death were about to close over her. Louder and louder she heard the call: "Come home with me, my friend." And she responded with a resounding *yes*, the response to God that had become a habit with her. Looking beyond the wires and tubes she wore, I saw her as the bride bedecked to meet her bridegroom. As the psalmist says: "All glorious is the King's daughter as she enters." (45:14) Her beauty is within.

This too was a journey that promised "great expectations." But this time, I am sure, there were no disappointments, no promises unfulfilled. It was a journey to the realm of perfect peace and boundless love. What eye has not seen nor ear heard nor human imagination ever dreamed of -- that she hears, that she sees, that she experiences. It is indeed beyond all expectations. As the poet puts it:

It was
As if I asked a common alms
And in my wondering hand
A stranger pressed a kingdom.

The death of a loved one -- and was there anyone more loved in this congregation than Marie Rene -- is always a reminder to all of us of our mortality and a call to reflect on that mortality, not in any morbid or fearsome way, but with the realization that, when this mortal life has passed, the bright promise of eternal life awaits us all. The death of a loved one gives special meaning to that prayer we have in the Eucharist just after the Lord's Prayer: "In your mercy keep us free from sin and protect us from all anxiety, as we wait in joyful hope for the coming of our saviour, Jesus Christ."

Our mortal life, here in the midst of God's people, has its meaning, its purposes and its responsibilities. And they are important. They demand our concern. But important as they are, they are penultimate, that is to say, they are not the ultimate concerns, but those that come before the ultimate. In ultimate terms our mortal life gives way to the bright promises of eternal life, as we hear whispered in our ear: "Come home, my friend. Come home to the life that is beyond all expectations. Your eyes will be full of seeing, your ears full of hearing, your heart full of love. You are my sisters and brothers. Where I am, there you also shall be. Yes, do come home with me, my friend."

SR. LIGUORI DUNLEA 12-3-1992

Readings: Job 19: 23-27
Philippians 3: 10-16
Matthew 16: 24-28

I have many memories of Sr. Liguori. One that comes to mind was an event that happened one Sunday some years ago, when I was saying Sunday Mass at the Infirmary. During the homily I had said something that people might consider a bit controversial. (I do that once in a while.) Anyway, at the end of the mass I said:

"During mass I had a holy distraction. The thought came to me that I sometimes say things in my homily that you might not agree with and, the way the liturgy is set up, you don't have any chance to respond or to question. Maybe I should come over once in a while during the week and give you the opportunity to have your say." I then went to the sacristy, took off the vestments, and left the chapel. Waiting at the door were three sisters, with Sr. Liguori at their head, saying: "When can you come?" And I did come for quite a few months and we had some interesting discussions. Sr. Liguori was always there and always had a question to ask or a comment to make.

Sr. Liguori was a fun-loving, happy person who had the hugest smile I have ever seen on anyone. When she was happy she was very, very happy and spread sunlight to others. But there were dark days, too, when she went through the experience of inner turmoil, when life seemed confusing, when God didn't seem to be there. We all know from experience that at times the sense of God's absence can seem very real. St. John of the Cross called it the dark night of the soul. But it is like the darkness that comes just before the dawn. After the darkness and the struggle with it, one discovers the true God and realizes that the God who was absent was not God at all but an idol. Some of us have to get rid of many idols before we meet the true God.

For Sr. Liguori there were times when even the true God seemed to be absent; but while God is never really absent, God is often hidden. And there are times, too, when God is elusive. And it is our task, no matter what the difficulties and sufferings may be, to find that hidden and elusive God. Sr. Liguori's search for that hidden and elusive God sometimes meant anguish and aching of spirit. She was not allowed to go around the valley of darkness. She had to go through it -- and more than once -- but she always knew in faith that, however hidden and elusive God might be, she would find God at the end of that journey through the dark valley; and when she reached there, she knew that God had been with her all the time, even though she had not always experienced the divine presence.

All of which is simply to say that her life was governed by the paschal mystery: the mystery of the dying and rising of Jesus. Through her baptism, Sr. Liguori entered into that paschal mystery. I speak about the paschal mystery because that is what Paul is talking about in our second reading. And I want to concentrate our reflection on that reading. My reason for this is that Sr. Liguori did not plan the liturgy for her funeral Mass. The only thing she said she wanted to be there for sure was this reading from Philippians 3: 10-16. It had special very meaning for her.

Her desire was the same as Paul's: "All I want to know is Christ and the power of the resurrection." She wanted to know and experience the paschal mystery of the Lord Jesus. Now, knowing the paschal mystery means knowing the road that Jesus took to arrive at that mystery. It was the Via Dolorosa the way of the cross. The sequence of the paschal mystery for Jesus was first the cross, and then the resurrection.

It's interesting to note that in the reading from Philippians, Paul reverses that process. He doesn't say: cross, then resurrection. Instead, he says: resurrection, then cross. Listen to what he says: "I want to share in the power of the resurrection of Jesus, so that I may share in His suffering."

Paul knew what he was talking about. We followers of Jesus are able to face the cross in our lives, because, in baptism which incorporates us into Christ and his paschal mystery, we have already experienced the power of the resurrection. We experience a victory gained not by us but for us. And it is a victory that no suffering can ultimately overcome. The power of the resurrection in us is always greater than the weight of the cross.

Sr. Liguori, though you were a person of joy with a witty sunny disposition, you suffered the weight of the cross many times in your life. It was pain and anguish for you. Yet you knew in faith, and deep down always believed, that there was a power working in you that was mightier than any suffering. The power of Christ's resurrection made it possible for you to live with the suffering and eventually to arrive at risen life. There were many deaths and resurrections in your life; but always it was the power of the resurrection of Jesus that opened the way to new life. Because of the power of the resurrection working in you, you were able, like Paul, to forget what was behind and, as he put it, to run ahead in order to grasp the prize to which God called you -- namely, life on high in Christ Jesus. But in trying to grasp Christ, you had the confident faith that you had already been grasped by him. Now we rejoice with you that you have finally been able to grasp him who so long ago grasped you in his love and in the power of his paschal mystery. We rejoice with you that there is no more suffering, no more pain, only the fullness of joy in God's presence.

I searched for a way to sum up Sr. Liguori's story: her simplicity, her deep faith and love for God, and also her experience at times of the hiddenness of God. I found what it think is an appropriate verse in Thomas Merton's poetry:

Her virtues, with their simple strings,
Play to the Lover hidden in the universe.

As we celebrate Sr. Liguori's victory – or, better, her sharing in Christ's victory -- we can be sure that in heaven's glory her virtues in all their wondrous simplicity play ever more eloquently to her Lover. But that Lover is no longer hidden. For now she sees God face to face.

SR.LUMINA KREGAR 8-24-1992

Readings: Job 22: 26-30
Philippians 3: 8-14
Matthew 11: 25-30

I never really came to know Sr. Lumina, though I often wished that I could get to know her. She was shy, I think, and probably a bit diffident about any contact with a priest. When she saw me coming, she tended to take off in the opposite direction. I do, however, remember two conversations I had with her. One was at a Christmas party of mine. Sr. Josette it was, I believe, who persuaded her to come. I recall inviting her to have a glass of Asti Spumante and she tasted it and said: "That is good."

The other occasion when we talked took place in the dining room. It happened that we were both picking up food. One of the items was pork chops. I put one on my plate. She looked at my plate and quickly shook her head. She pointed to the pork chop container and said to me: "Take two." For the moment at least she had forgotten any fear of me. She was in command. And I was suddenly transported back to my grade school days. I was suddenly a little boy again. I said: "Yes, Sister," and meekly took the second pork chop.

"Take two." I want to see these simple words as an expression of Sr. Lumina's life and of her spirituality. She was a woman of true Christian simplicity, An intelligent woman who never really was given the opportunity to develop the latent gifts she had. She was a lay sister at a time when their status was clearly below that of the other sisters. She did menial tasks and did them with a spirit of commitment and generosity. She was a kind of icon of the spirituality of the vast majority of us: the spirituality of the ordinary. Most of us will achieve life's goal not by doing anything very spectacular, but by doing the ordinary tasks of life with the same kind of commitment and generosity that Sr. Lumina exhibited in her life.

And that commitment and generosity were embodied in those two words: "Take two." For "take two" is the model of a spirituality that is ready to give to God more than God asks of us. It's a spirituality that reaches out to meet doubly the needs of our dear neighbor. It's a spirituality of doing more than is asked and going beyond what is needed. "Take two" is the spirituality of going the extra mile and giving the extra garment. I understand that Sr. Lumina liked on occasion to eat out. But she was always the one who wanted to pay for the meal for her company. When the bill came, it was her wish to pay all. She wanted to pay more than her share.

What I am suggesting is that those words which Sr. Lumina spoke to me in the dining room were not simply an isolated gesture. They go to the very heart of the charism of the Sisters of St. Joseph. For "take two" is one way of articulating that willingness always to do "the more" for God and for the good neighbor that has been part of your (our) charism from the very beginning. Sr. Lumina may not have had the opportunities for growth that many other sisters had, but she had a special grace -- the grace of the Holy Spirit -- that led her intuitively into the deepest understanding of the meaning of the vows she took as a religious and the charism of the congregation. St. Paul says, in the Epistle to the Galatians: "If we live by the Spirit, let us be guided by the Spirit." It is surely no mere coincidence that Sr. Lumina's chosen feast day was Pentecost: the feast of our life in the Spirit.

I have said many times on the occasion of funerals that a liturgy of this kind is more for us the living than for the dead. Sr. Lumina we can confidently commit to the mercy and love of our God, and believe that she who was blind now sees God face to face and she who was deaf now hears the music of the heavenly spheres. But we need to come here for our own sakes: to renew our commitment to the vocation that we have chosen as our way of living the life of the Spirit. The spirituality of "take two," the spirituality of doing more than is asked, of giving more than is required, is, indeed, the charism of this congregation. In fact, it is the call of every Christian who takes Faith seriously. Perfecting this spirituality of "take two," of "giving the more," is finally to achieve Christian maturity. Paul speaks of working toward such an achievement in a striking passage in Philippians, where he says: "I have not already attained to perfect maturity, but I press on hoping that I may possess it." He goes on to say that, letting go of what is behind, he presses on toward that goal. The word for "pressing on," *epectasis,* means seeking ever to do more and more. It means never quite achieving that goal, yet never ceasing from pressing on toward it.

Sr. Lumina has achieved the fullness of what is expressed by the spirituality of "the more." In this we rejoice. And her attainment spurs us on to press more ardently toward a goal that seems so elusive, but which we shall never cease to strive for. And the day will come when each of us shall achieve it fully, not here but in life immortal, where we will be with our dear sister, Lumina. May she rest in peace.

SR. BENEDICT MAHONEY 8-19-1992

Readings: Ezekiel 36: 24-28
Philippians 2: 6-11
Luke 1: 39-54

Sister Benedict, I am glad you waited to die long enough to give me time to come home so that I could keep the promise I made to you: to give the homily at your funeral liturgy. Actually, I made that promise several times. But the last time was on your feast day - July 11, the day I visited you on my return from a retreat in Dubuque. I remember that day. You said you weren't afraid to die. In fact you said that you were ready to die. Once again you told me that I was to preach at your funeral. But you warned me: "Don't you dare have any liturgical dance at my Mass or I'll trip them all."

Now you have done what you said you weren't afraid to do: you have said your total "yes" to God. And, in that spiritual body which Paul says we will have in risen life, God has given you a new heart. You'll never have heart failure again. You'll never again have a heart that works only part time. For, from now on, it will be the very heart of God that will beat within you.

Bennie -- I confess I find Bennie coming to my lips easier than Benedict -- though it was the other way around with you: you found it easier to say "Monsignor" than to say "Bill." You did try, though, and you managed it once in a while. I remember the first time. You had come in to talk about something with me. As you were leaving, you said: "Thank you, Monsignor." Then you stopped at the door and made yourself say: "I mean, thank you, Bill." And, in a very typical gesture, you covered your mouth with your hand and off you went. Then it became a little more frequent and I was glad. For, as I said, I find it easier to say "Bennie" to you. And I was happy that you were able to be on a first-name relationship with me.

Actually when you think about it, being able to name people by the names that best express who they are is an important aspect of friendship and relationships. Being able to name God is an important aspect of our relationship, our friendship, with God. There is a book by a Sufi master called *The Ninety-nine Names of God*. The point of the book is that God has a hundred names. There are ninety-nine that we are able to say. But there is one name that is secret and mysterious. It is a name we cannot say in this life. It is the name that God tells us when we enter fully into God's presence.

It is no exaggeration to say that all through our lives our spirituality consists in trying to say God, in learning to name God. And naming God is never just a matter of finding inclusive language to speak about God. It is something far deeper, far more mysterious. It is saying that hundredth name of God, which we can never say in this life, but only in eternity. Sister Benedict, on the feast of our Lady's assumption, experienced that God had done great things to her. For, at long last, she had been able to say the name of God: that name that can be known only by those who have entered fully into the heart of God.

Bennie, on August 15 you became a theologian. For it is the theologian's task to try to name God. And no theologian has ever been able to do that in this life. You used to come to me to discuss theological questions. Now you comprehend the truth and the wisdom that every theologian seeks. Now it is I who can come to you with questions. Now you know ever so much more about God than I could ever tell you.

Bennie, you who used to shake your head at me when I mentioned women priests, now, Bennie, I'm asking you: Haven't you found out that God has no problem about this at all? You used to be conservative in your thinking. Now, I ask you, isn't it true that in God there are no labels; in God there is neither male nor female, neither conservative nor liberal? Rather, all our differences are resolved, not dissolved or taken away, but resolved in that oneness with God which alone ultimately matters. God is great enough to include with the divine reality all our differences and contradictions and make them somehow come out right.

Then, Bennie, there is that matter of Ollie North whom you defended so vigorously and tenaciously. Do you still think his hands were clean in the Iran-Contra affair or are you now praying for his enlightenment?

There are many things I shall remember about Sr. Benedict. I shall remember her many kindnesses to me. Her kindnesses, for instance, when she ran the dining room and often filled my morning with the aroma of sizzling bacon and my evenings with pieces of choice carrot cake. Most of all, I will remember her facial expressions. I was delighted to see the beautiful photograph on her casket. It captures beautifully her smile. And she was at her best when that smile lighted up her face. But there were other facial expressions that depicted other moods in her. When she scowled at something she didn't like, you knew she was scowling. And when she was delighted with something, her eyes opened up widely, like the eyes of a lovely, innocent child. When she was serious about something, the gravity of her look showed the importance of the matter at hand. But most of all, her face expressed so often the concern and the care of a loving heart. Though the heart of her body slowly began to function less and less effectively, the heart of her spirit never ceased to go out in concern for those who were dear to her and for all those who were in need.

Sr. Benedict's name has already gone up on the board outside the south side door of the chapel. On that board there are now listed 844 names of sisters. When we refer to that board, we say: "These are the sisters who have died." And this is right, but we should always add: "Because they have died, they are the sisters who are really alive, fully alive. They are the great theologians of our congregation. For they are able to name God. They can say the inexpressible Name, whose saying brings the greatest possible joy and happiness."

We, by contrast with these 844 sisters, are each day experiencing a little bit of dying, as we move toward that day when we shall join them in the fullness of true life in God. Meanwhile, we can look at that board and see the names of those who are able to name God. They were people who once lived, with varying degrees of unity and communion, in community as Sisters of St. Joseph. Now they live in full communion with God and with one another. Today, as we look at that board, we realize that we see before our eyes one of the great doctrines of our faith. It is a doctrine we express our belief in every time we say, in the Creed: "I believe in the communion of saints." Yes, these sisters listed on the Board are the sisters of the Magnificat. For "the Lord has done great things for them and holy is God's name."

On late Sunday afternoon I like to watch the golf matches on television. At tournament they have what is called "the leader board." It lists the names of all the players, with the leaders on top. That board outside the chapel is our "leader board." It's a board on which all are leaders. It holds the names of those who lead us on the way to the fulfillment of our human journey. For all of us who love her, it is a joy to see Bennie's name affixed to our "leader board."

Farewell, dear friend. And may flights of angels wing thee to thy rest!

SR. WILMA JOSEPH OSBORNE 6-17-1992

Readings: 2 Kings 2: 9-11
Romans 14: 7-12
Luke 12: 35-40

I was 2500 miles away, giving a retreat at the Shalom Center in Portland, Oregon, when Sr. Mary Paul called me to tell me about Sr. Wilma Joseph's death. I was shocked, as I am sure all of you were, and very much wished that I could have been at home to share with you in the sorrow and bewilderment of so sudden a death. Mary Paul's call came just as I was about to give a presentation on God's love for us as unconditional love. And it was a comfort to me to think: Now Wilma could give this talk so much better than I, for now she knows more about this than I can possibly say. For she has entered into that unconditional love, when on Saturday --so unexpectedly-- she died into God.

I thought of her too, as yesterday I took the plane that brought me back from Portland to Rochester. As we headed heavenward and climbed and climbed to some 37,000 feet, I thought to myself: in Wilma's Mass, we must use the reading from Second Kings about Elijah ascending to heaven in a fiery chariot. What better story to symbolize the return to God of one who kept all our chariots in working order?

Something else too about this trip home. We passed through storms on the way from Portland and were delayed in getting into Chicago. I got off the plane at five minutes to eight and mounted my chariot, the wheelchair that was waiting for me. The Rochester plane was leaving at eight o'clock. I said a prayer to Wilma:

"Get me to the plane on time." I told the man pushing the chair: "I have to be at gate 30 in five minutes." It was at the far end of the concourse. He said: "No problem. " And I remembered how many times Wilma had said that to me when, with a look of in feigned helplessness on my face, I asked her to do something with my car: "No problem." We got there just as they were about to close the door for departure. And I said: "Thanks, Wilma. You saved me again. You're only a couple of days in that full presence of God and already we have your first miracle!"

As I was flying home I thought to myself: "What can I possibly say at this liturgy of Christian burial for her?" Death has gathered us into this chapel many times. Most always it's for a death that has been expected, waited for -- by someone begging God to take her into the fullness of God's life. On such occasions, even when there may be a deep feeling of loss, there is an all-pervading joy. We believe in eternal life. We believe that our sister, who awaited death, has gone through death's door into the fullness of God's holy presence.

But tonight, our emotions are much more complicated. Somewhere among them is this sense of joy that Wilma has come to the goal of the journey she began with her baptism into Christ. But this feeling is clouded over by other emotions. There is the shock, still present, that it all happened so quickly. We can be sure she was prepared (maybe even expecting it more than she let on), but we were not at all prepared. And there are questions, too, questions we cannot and should not suppress: "Why did this happen? Why was she taken now when she still had so much more to continue to give to the congregation?" We try to answer: "God knows best." But that doesn't really shed any light on our bewilderment. For we don't really know what that means.

We believe, but we realize that faith doesn't really make things any clearer for us than they would be for those without faith. And this jolting experience helps us to realize what faith really is: it is often darkness rather than a light. And we understand the words of the poet: "Why is our God so often a serpent or a question mark?" We come to know that faith is not intended to be a crutch, but a strength. It's not a book where we can go to look up all the answers. Rather it's a place to stand. It gives us security, not comfort. It's a key that opens the door not to the secret of life, but to its mystery. Faith is hanging on to what Thomas Merton, in a celebrated passage in *Conjectures of a Guilty Bystander* calls the eschatological secret of Julian of Norwich. What she wrote about was a hidden dynamism that is at work in the world. We neither see it clearly nor understand it fully: it is a power working in our midst whereby " all manner of things shall be well." That secret is in God and is what Jesus brings when he comes to call us, as he came to Wilma Saturday night. For he comes with the final answer to the world's anguish. This is Julian's secret: our task in life is not to solve the contradictions and absurdities of life, but to live in the midst of them, knowing that the secret, that can never be guessed at, will be revealed. But the key to the secret is not something we hold, but something that Christ brings us when we comes, as he came to Wilma Saturday night. She knows now the secret: that "all will be well. You shall see." She would tell us now, "that all shall be well, that all manner of things shall be well."

I am sure that one of the reasons Sr. Wilma Joseph's death was such a shock was that her ministry touched practically every one in the congregation. She was the queen of the journey who made sure that all would be well when people went on a journey, whether they were going to a ministry, a retreat, a convention, a vacation. Now this queen of the journey has taken her own final journey. It was the journey of but an instant, for sitting in her chair in her room she quite simply traveled into God and died into the fullness of God's presence.

She loved fun. She planned pool parties. (I even got to one!) She played the role of Santa Claus at Christmas. She loved to watch the sunset - occasionally with a beer in her hands. And she loved the deer that are so plentiful on our property. It is so appropriate that the responsorial psalm in our liturgy is one which compares the person yearning for God to a deer yearning for running waters.

About a week or so ago, I drove through the motherhouse gate just after dusk and in the grass on the north side of the road, but close to the road, was a deer grazing. I stopped the car and looked at this beautiful creature. The deer looked up at me and then turned back to her grazing. Her every movement was completely lovely and there was a kind of gaucheness about these movements that made her even lovelier, like the beauty in the awkwardness of an adolescent girl. I wanted to reach out and touch the softness of her brown coat. And, on reflection I saw something in the deer -- something most wonderful, something beyond the trivialities of every day existence. Something deep and profound. The Face of that which is in the deer and in me and in all of us. What Wilma saw, truly but obscurely in the beauty of the deer, she now sees face to face. She was the deer yearning for the streams of living water, the soul thirsting for God. She has found their source. She knows for herself whence comes the beauty of the deer. She knows for herself that all things are well; and, as one who always took so much pleasure in doing nice things for people, she wants us to know that "all manner of things shall be well." She would tell those who are willing to listen that there is a level of consciousness which is present in all of us, a level of consciousness at which all the contradictions, ambiguities and absurdities of life are resolved. We have extraordinary moments in this life when we achieve, if only for a brief moment, this level of consciousness. Wilma has achieved this wondrous and joyous reality -- not for a fleeting moment, but for an eternity.

Let us praise God for her ministry among us. Let us praise God for the glory God has given her in God's holy Presence.

Farewell to you, Wilma, keeper of the keys. Farewell to you, queen of the journey.

SR. ST. TERESA ROCHE 7-27-1988

Readings: Revelation 21: 1-7
John 14: 1-6

It is always something of a jolt to me to go to the St. Joseph's Convent and Infirmary on Sunday and find that someone to whom I had been giving Communion for a long time is no longer there. That was my experience Last Sunday, as I went to the second floor and did not see Sr. St. Teresa in her usual position — in a chair just outside the choirloft. As I think of her, I can remember her moving from the chapel, to the choir, to the hall outside the choir—Loft on the second floor. Then Sunday she was not there. Though I knew she had died, it still is something of a shock to you when what has become very familiar suddenly ceases to happen, when someone you have been accustomed to see, you see no longer.

As I reflect on Sr. St. Teresa, I can remember an expression that gradually came to identify her for me: a gaze that seemed hardly to see what was ahead of her, coupled with a gentle smile that spoke a sense of inwardness. Her face never seemed drawn or tense. It was calm and peaceful. One had the sense that, if she seemed to be losing contact with the reality that was outside her, there was a mystery in her look that suggested her heart was discovering more and more the Reality that was within — discovering that "Inward Stranger" whom she had never seen, but whom, in her silence, she was perhaps experiencing in a way she had never experienced Him before.

When someone goes through the experience of Alzheimer's disease or some similar disability, that person becomes more and more withdrawn from the external and the superficial reality outside. Seeing this happen can be painful to those who love this person. Yet we must not forget that it is precisely such external and superficial realities that so often prevent us from experiencing the deep inner reality that is our true self: our true identity before God and in God. I cannot help but think that, in the loving mercy of God, for those to whom this happens the loss of the outward becomes a gain of what is inward. We know how, with the best will in the world, we are continually being distracted from any kind of total attentiveness to what is within because perforce we are so constantly dealing with what is without.

Someone whose contact with exterior reality has become more and more minimal may well find herself discovering the depths and the beauty of an inner world, where one can meet God in the deepest possible personal encounter. There is a whole world of inward beauty that we catch glimpses of at time, but which, we can surely say, Sr. St. Teresa, as she moved more and more inward, discovered in a way that perhaps most of us have yet to do. Did she, without ever speaking externally about it, have on the lips of her heart the words of the poet?

Closer and clearer
Than any wordy master,
Thou inward Stranger
Whom I have never seen.
Deeper and cleaner
Than the clamorous ocean
Seize up my silence
Hold me in thy Hand.

That Inward Stranger, whom she saw in the depths of her being in the silence of the last months of her life, she now sees face to face. He is no longer Stranger. In a mysterious way we cannot understand, He is her other self. She is totally in Him. What joy! The Word has shattered her silence. She has entered into that ocean of divine Mercy that is the wondrous Reality of God. She is held forever in the shelter of His Hand.

I was thinking, as I reflected on this liturgy for Sr. St. Teresa's Mass, that my own life can be, in some sense, divided into two parts: the first part, in which I was college chaplain and spent most every Saturday (at least during the summer) officiating at weddings of Nazareth alumnae, celebrating with them the seventh of the sacraments. Then there is the second part, in which I have found myself frequently presiding at liturgies of Christian burial, celebrating what I like to call the eighth and greatest of the sacraments: the sacrament of death.

All this has been a salutary experience for me. Reflecting on death, trying to understand the mystery of it all, and at last coming to see it as a sacrament has been for me an experience of great growth. It has been the discovery of joy in what we often see only as sorrow, and gain in what we often see only as loss.

I venture to say that this is not only my experience, but yours also. As you gather so many times to say farewell to beloved sisters and to commend them confidently to God, I am sure that you have reflected on death's meaning and have come to see it as Christian faith calls us to see it: namely, not as an end but a beginning, not a closure to life, but an entrance into a kind of life that even our wildest dreams cannot imagine.

That this should happen to you and me is a great good. For it surely is true that the celebration of a liturgy of Christian burial is more for us than for the deceased. What wondrous things Sr. St. Teresa could tell, if she were at this lectern instead of me. She knows now the true, rapturously joyful reality that death is, that death ushers us into. She knows what it means to live life immortal, as something so totally different from what we call life that we almost need a different word to describe it. What she now knows by experience, we have come to believe in the firmness of that faith that comes from the Risen Jesus. Each funeral we celebrate deepens that faith: it draws us into an appreciation of this eighth sacrament. That is why I say that what we do here this evening is more for us than for her.

So we come together tonight to celebrate Sr. St. Teresa's return to her God, but we come also because her death can help us to see the side of death that is pure darkness for so many people, but is a wondrous light for us when we view death through faith's eyes. It's this faith picture that is in the book of Revelation: no more tears, no more mourning or crying out, no more pain; everything made new!

In the Gospel Jesus tells us that he wants us to be where he is. In a sense we are where he is, because as the Risen One He is always at our side. Yet on this side of death, we never have the totality of awareness that He is really there. Let us rejoice that this totality of awareness is already enjoyed by Sr. St. Teresa. And let us not be afraid to await, with a kind of quiet joy, this moment in our own lives. May we make our own the prayer we say every day in the Eucharist: "Protect us from all anxiety, as we wait in joyful hope the coming of our Saviour, Jesus Christ."

SR. GEMMA MARIE CAMMILLERI 3-17-2005

Ecclesiastes 3:1-8
Eph 1:3-10
Jn 15:9-17

Someone said last night that Sr. Gemma Marie liked to laugh (and I remember her laughter and her smile). Wouldn't she have enjoyed the fact that she is the center of attention on – of all days – St. Patrick's Day? That on this day beloved of all the Irish, we gather to celebrate the life of an Italian nun. Yet when you reflect a bit more deeply, you realize that this is quite right. After all, doesn't Paul say that because of Christ we are no longer Jew or Gentile, free or slave, male or female, Irish or Italian? We are all one in Christ Jesus.

And that oneness is a wonderful reality: for it doesn't blur or erase our differences; rather it brings them together into a harmonious blending that preserves and accentuates the richness and the beauty of all God's people. That is what we mean by the marvelous, many-colored reality that we call the communion of saints.

On Tuesday Sr. Gemma Marie died into God. What was significant about her death was not what it terminated, but what it inaugurated. Her death ended the mortal phase of her existence and began the immortal phase of that existence that will last forever in joy and peace and glory. Her death was but a momentary interruption of a human existence that God willed should have no end.

Qoheleth, who wrote our first reading, was a died-in-the-wool pessimist. For him everything was "vanity and chasing after wind." Still, listening to him, one quickly comes to realize that, pessimist though he was, he was a great writer: he had a wonderful ability in putting words together so beautifully. Probably no text in the Hebrew Scriptures is more often quoted that the words of our reading:

> For everything there is a season
> and a time for everything under heaven:
> a time to be born and a time to die…
> a time to weep and a time to laugh…
> a time to keep silence and a time to speak.

What Qoheleth could not have known, but what we know – with the certainty of faith – is that *there is a reality beyond time*: the reality of God's everlasting life that we are born to share in: the wonderful reality of the communion of saints.

As many of you know, Elizabeth Johnson, a CSJ from Brentwood, has written a splendid book about the communion of saints. At a funeral liturgy it is timely and appropriate – maybe even necessary -- for us to reflect on the communion of saints.

It is a significant fact that in the First World, since the Second Vatican Council, devotion to the saints has experienced an extraordinary and unfortunate decline. In the Third World, however, -- as our sisters in Brazil know so well – an oppressed people have reclaimed the saints as partners in their struggle against oppression.

In a age marked by an excessive individualism and a crass consumerism – that can think only in terms of this-world realities -- we need to recover that sense of clear and easy trafficking between heaven and earth enjoyed by our early Christian and medieval ancestors, as well as by our sisters and brothers in the developing countries.

We need to think of the communion of saints as a communion of equal companions in grace that extends across the world, that is impervious to time and that is beyond death. We need to move, Elizabeth Johnson suggests, from a patron-client approach to the saints that builds on a patriarchal model and move to an egalitarian approach that sees all those graced by God, living on both sides of death, as companions, or -- in the words of the book of wisdom -- as :friends of God and prophets.

More often than we think, it happens that people, especially toward the end of their lives, have a stronger and stronger sense of the bonds that link us with that other world that is our true home, toward which we have been journeying all our lives. Must we not believe that in those last days of her mortal existence, Sr. Gemma was close to that other world and in a special way to her dear friend, Sr. Mary Paschal?

The communion of saints must not be simply a truth we give assent to because it is in the Creed. It is an experience that can be ours, a source of joy and peace that comes from our realization that death brings not separation, but communion: we are united with our loved ones who have gone to God. For they are in God and we are in God.

Much of our thinking and speaking about death has been influenced by an unfortunate dualism that has plagued Christian thought for centuries. Because of this, we have to purify much of the language we use in speaking about death. Last night at the wake service, we prayed: Sr. Gemma Marie "is gone now from this earthly dwelling and has left behind those who mourn her absence."

Is Sr. Gemma Marie really absent from us? Where is she? Surely we will answer that she is in God. But so are we in God (for God is everywhere). If she is in God and we are in God, how can we think of her as absent from us? Karl Rahner, one of the architects of Vatican II has written:

> The great and sad mistake of many people – among them even pious persons – is to imagine that those whom death has taken leave us. They do not leave us. They remain! Where are they? In darkness? Oh no! It is we who are in darkness. We do not see them, but they see us. Their eyes, radiant with glory, are fixed upon our eyes full of tears. Oh infinite consolation! Though invisible to us, our dead are not absent.

A few minutes ago, as I moved from the vestry to the chapel, I passed the board that lists the names of all our beloved sisters who have entered into that full awareness of God that we call heaven. As I looked upon that board, I asked them: "May we join you in song?" Later in the preface of the Mass, I will put this in a more formal way: "So with all the choirs of angels and saints we proclaim your glory and join in their unending hymn of praise." Then we do join them in the Holy Holy Holy.

Yes, Gemma is with us. So are they. We do indeed touch heaven – more than we realize.

SR. BLANCHE BOSSERT 7-22-1990

Readings: Rom. 8: 31-35, 37-39
Lk. 12: 35-40

It was only the other day, after her death, that I learned that Sister Blanche and I had taught together. Well, sort of. I just learned that she was Sr. Agnes Regina who taught the second grade at least part of the time I was stationed at Sacred Heart. She had to put up with me coming into her grade each week. I was supposed to teach them religion. But the thought of teaching theology to children of that age terrified me. So I told them ghost stories instead. Sister probably had to get them quieted down after I departed.

She was a lovely, gentle woman and a fine teacher. But in the last dozen or more years of her life, everything changed. Sr. Blanche became like one of the women in the parable waiting for the master to come. He came twice to her in these last years. First he came to her in the terrible day of her suffering. He came to give her the cross, the most difficult cross of all: the cross that comes with the inability to communicate with others.

He came a second time to her -last Sunday, when he came to bring her to himself, to bring her the eternal joy and happiness that she had so long awaited: the joy of risen life.

Sr. Blanche, in her late years, modeled for all of us a virtue much prized in the Gospels, but now almost forgotten as a virtue. I speak of the virtue of waiting. There are times in our lives when we are called to action; and we must act. And there are times when we are called to what may be more difficult -- simply to wait. It is important for our spiritual well-being that we realize that the waiting is not just putting in time. The waiting itself has meaning.

In the hurried, frenzied culture in which we live it is difficult to see waiting as anything better than a chore. Waiting taxes our patience. We wait in a traffic line because there is an accident up ahead. We wait in a supermarket, because there were so many insensitive people who decided to shop at the same time we did. Children wait to get through grade school, so that they can get to high school; then they wait this out so they can get to college. Then they wait for that life of independence which they suppose comes after college. We wait for a friend to come to visit us and are anxious because the friend is late. We wait for the flu bug to leave our system so that we can carry on our lives as usual.

So much of life is waiting, and so often the waiting means nothing more than frustration. "Waiting" is something we have to put up with. It has to be endured.

But there is another kind of waiting. There is the waiting of a mother for her child to be born, and that waiting is the joy of life growing within her. There is the waiting of a writer for an inarticulate idea that has come to his/her mind to be formed finally into a clear and forceful statement. The waiting for the plot to unfold, as we read an absorbing story. Waiting for a son or daughter or a niece or nephew or the child of a friend to grow up to the maturity that the brightness of youth promises. There is the waiting for the right answer to a question, as I begin to grasp the elements of the question and as my struggling with them moves me in the direction of the answer; but for the fullness of the answer, I shall have to wait.

This type of waiting is not the "waiting of frustration"; on the contrary, it is a waiting of joyous expectation. It is not just time to be put in but time to be enjoyed. Such waiting is to be reveled in. For the joy of expectation participates in the joy of fulfillment. Part of the joy of a trip is planning it. Part of the joy of getting to a destination is the journey that gets you there. This is the kind of waiting that belongs to the liturgical season of Advent. We await the Lord's coming with the realization that He is already in our midst; but since we are not fully aware of His Presence, we have to wait for our own consciousness to catch up with reality. But the waiting is living with the Mystery that is to come. It is watching it unfold. It is readying the atmosphere which makes that unfolding possible. Waiting is sinking into the meaning of the Mystery.

There is a poem by R. S. Thomas the Anglican priest and Welsh poet whom I often refer to, which captures this understanding of that waiting which is pregnant with meaning. In the poem entitled "Kneeling," he pictures himself kneeling before an altar just before he is to preach. There is a silence in the air, like a staircase from heaven. Sunlight rings the preacher as he kneels, just before he takes on his role as God's spokesperson. He asks God to prompt him in what he says; yet even though God speaks through him, he realizes only too well -- as every preacher must -- that something will be lost. People will have to wait. It will take time for God's meaning to sink into their hearts. But the meaning will emerge from the waiting.

> Moments of great calm,
> Kneeling before an altar
> Of wood in a stone church
> In summer, waiting for the God
> To speak; the air a staircase
> For silence; the sun's light
> Ringing me, as though I acted
> A great role. And the audiences
> Still; all that close throng
> Of spirits waiting, as I,
> For the message.
> Prompt me, God;
> But not yet. When I speak,
> Though it be you who speak
> Through me, something is lost.
> The meaning is in the waiting.
> (Poems, 1946-1968 p. 119)

For the last dozen years, Sr. Blanche's life was a life of waiting. She had lost the conscious power to communicate with people around her. But we must remember that there is more to us than the conscious realm of pure being. There are the unconscious and the super conscious realms of our reality. It is especially at these

- 238 -

levels that we can achieve the deepest contact with God. Indeed, we are so often occupied with the conscious level of our being that we never reach into the deeper recesses of our reality where alone we can find God as God truly is.

If people who lose one of their senses acquire a deeper sensitivity in their other senses, does it not seem reasonable for us to think that, when Sr. Blanche lost any real contact with her conscious reality, there was nothing to distract her from experiencing God at those deeper levels of our being that we don't often reach, because we are so engrossed at the level of superficial consciousness? Is it not reasonable to think that, in those long years of waiting for the return of her Lord and Master, she was experiencing God at a depth we can scarcely appreciate? Was she, who could not communicate with us, communicating with God at a very deep level, saying: "Out of the depths I cry to you, O Lord. Lord hear my voice. Be attentive to me."

Of course, it is hard for us to think this way. We are so easily tempted to think of such years of waiting as wasted years as we wonder what possible meaning they could have. And perhaps Blanche, who is now one with God at the deepest possible level, would answer us and say:

"The meaning was in the waiting. I was waiting for the Lord who had come once with crucifixion and whom I knew would one day come with resurrection. My soul trusted in the Lord. My soul waited for the Lord. More than sentinels wait for the dawn, I waited for the Lord to come and fulfill his promises to me. And I have not waited in vain. There was meaning in the waiting——a meaning whose fullness I know only now."

SR. MARY CAROLINE DONOHUE 11-23-1992

Readings: Ezechiel 34: 11-16
Jn. 10: 11-18

At two o'clock last Wednesday, Sr. Mary Caroline took her last ride on lift line. This time it was a heavenly one that lifted her all the way up to the very throne of God. One can almost picture her arriving (and surely it had to be in her cart); and, with that big grin that she could sometimes show on her face, looking all around and saying: "Well, here I am."

I'm sure she left the cart behind. But it's hard not to think of her in that ever present cart. One day, when I visited her, she had me in stitches, as she recounted her first and last drive with a new cart. She had just gotten it and was trying it out. She went into the community room at the infirmary. A number of sisters were there. All at once Sr. Mary Caroline pushed a button and the machine got completely out of control. It was circling around the community room, like a bucking bronco, going every which way. As she careened around the room, the other sisters in the room were moving this way and that to get out of her way. Fortunately, she did not run into anyone. But, as she told me the story, I could only picture sisters scurrying this way and that, moving much faster than they had done in a long while, as Mary Caroline and her unruly steed circled dizzily around the room. She was finally corralled by a table that she ran into that mercifully stopped the machine. Even though she was banged up herself by this strange adventure, she was grateful that no one else had been hurt. Though she told me the story in a very serious tone, she had that twinkle of laughter in her eyes. She knew it was an hilarious story and she enjoyed telling it.

I am sure she didn't arrive in heaven that way. And I say that because I know that she had mastered the way of the journey toward God in a way she had not mastered that route around the community room.

As you all know, Sr. Mary Caroline endured a great deal of suffering and severe pain in her last years. But there is a part of the story of her last years that not many know about; and it's the story that really matters: the story of her spiritual growth. When I first began seeing her regularly, I talked with her about contemplation. At first she didn't believe that this was ever for the likes of her. We talked a good deal about it and she read about it. Then one day when I visited her, she told me that she had been in severe pain much of the night before. But this time it had been different. Instead of almost despairing till the night would be over, she said: "When I wasn't sleeping, I spent my time in contemplative prayer and I felt that God was there." From then on that was her story: not a lessening of pain, but a quiet growth in the awareness of God's presence. More and more she could identify with Merton's poem "The Stranger," in which he says, in part:

> Closer and clearer
>
> Than any wordy master,
>
> Thou inward Stranger
>
> Whom I have never seen.
>
> Deeper and cleaner
>
> Than the clamorous ocean
>
> Seize up my silence
>
> Hold me in thy Hand!

In the silence and solitude that brought not only pain but also presence, she was taught by that "inward Stranger."

> If you seek a heavenly light
>
> I Solitude, am your professor!
>
> I go before you into emptiness
>
> Raise strange suns for your new mornings
>
> Opening the windows
>
> Of your inmost apartment...
>
> Follow my ways and I will lead you
>
> To golden-haired suns
>
> Logos and music, blameless joys,

Innocent of questions

And beyond answers.

For I, Solitude, am thine own self

I, Nothingness, am thy All.

I, Silence, am thy Amen!

That sense of God's presence brought a peace and a quiet to her -- but not completely. There was yet another step she had to take before she could let herself go fully into the arms of God. She had to overcome the almost morbid fear of death that she had. She once said to me: "I hear the talks you give at sisters' funerals. You speak about death as a beautiful experience. But, even though I try, I just can't accept that. I am afraid to die."

And we talked about it and I tried to suggest that accepting our own death was really the final fruit of contemplation. Contemplation is yielding oneself to God for a period of time. Death is yielding oneself to God forever, for all eternity. She so wanted to believe and all I could say was: pray and God will give you the faith to believe. We talked many times about that.

And that gift was given to her. And she confided that to her lifelong friend, Mother Agnes Cecilia. Mother stopped in to see her just two days before she died. All mechanical hook-ups had been removed. Mother said to her: "I'm so glad all that stuff has been taken away. Your eyes look good. You look like your old self." Sr. Mary Caroline smiled at her and said: "Agnes, all that glitters is not gold." (Can't you just hear her saying that?) Mother said to her: 'Are you telling me something? Are you saying that you aren't going to make it?" She answered: "Yes. But it's all right. I am resigned to it. I am ready." And when Sr. Rosemary St. Peter (whose many kindnesses to her Sr. Mary Caroline appreciated so much) visited her, she was able to say: "I am at peace with God. I am at peace with my family. I am at peace with the congregation."

How wonderful that she, who for so long a time seemed unable to experience that peace, could make those statements, as she moved ever more closely into the full presence of God.

The readings for this liturgy were all her choice. They are so appropriate. They center about the theme of the Good Shepherd, who loves his sheep and leads them, sometimes through the valley of darkness, to the green pastures of God's peace and light. In her last days, Sr. Mary Caroline was at peace, because that Inward Stranger, her Good Shepherd, had taught her not to be afraid. For the Good Shepherd knows the sheep and they follow that Shepherd wherever he leads. On November 18, 1992, her fears were gone. She knew the love of the One who would lay down his life for his friends. She knew at last -- what she was never quite certain about for so long a time -- that she was indeed in that circle of friends. She had the grace and the courage to follow him wherever he led. And He led her to that full possession of God's Presence. Nothing now can ever separate her from Christ. She is one with him and he with her. She who was often without rest in body and spirit, now has eternal rest and all we can do is praise God, who has done such wondrous things for her. Holy is God's name.

SR. VERONICA MARIE FREIDA 8-29-2005

Readings: Wis. 3:1-9
1 Jn. 3:1-3
Mt. 11: 25-30

      The long vigil of waiting at Sr. Veronica Marie's bedside finally came to an end Friday morning at 2:00 a.m. Fittingly, her ever faithful sister, Bernadine was present and with her as was her loyal friend Maria. They were there for so many hours and days and months. Friday morning at 2: 00 a.m. they witnessed a transformation as the place that for so long had been Calvary for Veronica Marie became for her the mountain of the Ascension. Bernadine and

Maria took leave of her, as she passed through the portals of death into the loving arms of the God she served so well.

Veronica did many wonderful and helpful things for me during the years she was in charge of the "priests' kitchen" and my rooms. She was one of the most generous persons I have ever known. No matter what you asked her to do, she was always willing and happy in doing it. It was almost as if you were doing her a favor by asking her assistance. I know also that she was delighted when my going on vacation gave her the opportunity of trying to create some kind of order out of chaos in my office. One of many things I especially remember about her was her swiftness in getting things done immediately and quickly. Actually, I believe that is a characteristic Freida trait. No matter what you asked her to do, you could be sure it would be done at once, if not sooner. She was never one to delay, to put things off.

That is why there was a certain irony in her death process. She -- who never delayed in doing things -- seemed to change character at the end and kept putting off the moment of her death. Time and time again we were sure that the moment had come, only to see her rally at the last moment. [Some of us suspected it was Father Bruce's doing, because everybody knows that when he blesses someone they always take a turn for the better.] Actually, we know she was not delaying; rather, she was waiting. Waiting for God's call. She learned the lesson of yesterday's Gospel that resurrection is preceded by suffering. Why it has to be this way –we simply do not know. What Veronica's sufferings were in those many months -- after she had lost practically all ability to communicate, except at times to nod "yes" or "no" – will always remain a mystery to us.

So often she stared off into space, as if she were seeing something in the distance: not so much on the wall, but somehow beyond it. At times the look on her face would be one of peace, and other moments it would be a look of anxiety and distress. At times she would nod her head "yes" or "no," when asked if what she saw was "good" or "bad." Were the bad images intimations of the suffering she was being asked to undergo? Were the good images assurances of God's presence with her through it all? As I say we cannot know. We can only reflect in wonder and awe at the mystery of a level of consciousness that, try as we will, will always defy our desire to understand it. All we can say is what the book of Wisdom says: "The souls of the righteous are in the hands of God...God tested her and found her worthy of himself; like gold in the furnace God tried her and like a sacrificial burnt offering God accepted her... [Therefore] she abides with him in love." Or as the second reading puts it: we are God's children in this life, but what that means in all its completeness will be revealed only when we pass into the fullness of God. Veronica is already there. She knows in all its fullness what it means to be a child of God.

Sr. Veronica Marie's life as a Sister of St. Joseph was not a spectacular story. In fact, it was – like the stories of most of us -- an ordinary story. She worked hard at whatever she was asked to do: whether it was altar breads or hospital records or the onerous task of caring for the Motherhouse chaplain. Oftentimes she was willing to do things that others did not particularly want to do. She was content to work in the background. She was one of God's beloved little ones portrayed in the Gospel. Her life was lived not in the limelight, but in the shadows. Now she understands the meaning of Milton's words: "What if earth be but the shadow of heaven and the things therein?" For now she lives the only life that is truly real and filled with wondrous peace and joy, where there are no shadows, only the fullness of light. Where God's holy ones are who have no need of lamp or sun. For the Lord God is their light forever.

I am sure many of you have seen the movie *Shadowlands.* It is the story of C. S. Lewis. The climax of the story shows this brilliant Oxford professor deeply distraught by the death of his beloved wife, Joy. In one poignant scene he sits on the back doorstep with his adopted son. The young lad says to him: "Jack, do you believe in heaven?" Lewis pauses for a while, then says: "Yes, I do." In a touching moment, the boy looks away from him and says: "I don't." In the days that follow the two of them take many quiet walks together. Then one day, Lewis says to the boy: "We live only in the shadow lands. Your mother lives the only life that is truly real and full of joy."

Sr. Veronica Marie now lives that life: the only life that is truly real and full of joy. She is in the light; we are in the shadowlands.

I know that Veronica would want me to say a word of heartfelt thanks from her to Bernadine for her selfless, loving care. Being older and, perhaps, more accomplished, she was something of a mother figure to Veronica. And especially in those last days, when I saw Bernadine looking so worn and tired, I could not help but think of the words of the *Stabat Mater*.

Stabat mater dolorosa   At the cross her station keeping
juxta crucem lacrimosa   stood the mournful sister weeping
dum pendebat filius.   close to Veronica Marie to the end.

As Mary stood beneath the cross of Jesus, there was with her another woman named Mary. With Bernadine there was always at her side her faithful friend, Maria. They

- 248 -

both remained close to Veronica to the very end and were able to close her eyes, as she gave up her spirit to God. It was so fitting and a wonderful grace for both of them to be there to the very end, ushering her into the presence of God – the God she loved and served so well, the God who finally called her to enter to joy of God's loving presence.

Sr. Edwarda McCarthy – 9-27-2005

Readings: Wis. 3:1-6
Rom. 5: 1-5
Jn. 15: 9-`7

"Sr. Edwarda, are you afraid to die?" I put this question to Edwarda not during time of her last illness, but one day four or five years ago when she and I were in a police patrol car being taken to the Fairport jail. I hasten to say that we were not under arrest. We had been asked to go to the jail to identify a man who had entered the Motherhouse with a gun – at the time when Edwarda was at the switch board. He was obviously a troubled man. He said to Edwarda: "I want to speak with your boss." Edwarda's calm reply was: "God is my boss." The would-be robber was bewildered. He hadn't bargained for this. His gun was no match for God. Meanwhile, Sr. Edwarda called

Mother Agnes Cecilia who in turn called the police and also me. The police came very quickly and an officer finally persuaded the man – who by this time was quite ready to hand himself over to a police officer whom he could see rather than deal with a God he could not see -- to hand over his gun. He was taken to the jail in Fairport and we were asked to go there too -- in another police car to identify him. On our way I put the question to Edwarda: "Did you think that he might kill you?" "Oh, yes," she said in a rather manner-of-fact sort of way. "Were you afraid?" "I don't think so," she said.

This brief episode illustrates the fact that, though her slight build may have suggested frailty, she was anything but frail in spirit and character. Besides being a most popular teacher of French – in various places and at various levels, as well as an accomplished cellist, she was – it gladdens my heart to say – a staunch and strong-willed Democrat. She read the newspapers carefully and listened to the newscasts to keep up with what was going on in the world. Nor was she slow to offer her evaluation of events as they happened.

The two words that come most quickly to me when I think of Edwarda are graciousness and gratefulness. There was a graciousness about her. An elegance. A dignity. There was a kindliness and a way of propriety about her. She knew what was expected of a lady. One might almost say that there is a sense in which she might have walked out of the pages of a Jane Austen novel. One saw in her a deep humility and the desire to be the best possible religious she could be. Yes, she was a gentle, gracious woman.

And then gratefulness – she was ever appreciative of a favor done to her. Many times, especially in those final days, I would go to her room and give her a blessing.

Invariably she would say "thank you" and "that is the best gift you could give me." And I am sure that there are many others here who heard her expressions of gratitude.

Graciousness and gratefulness – both are closely connected with the word "grace." I want to say that Sr. Edwarda lived a graced life. And I am sure that you would all agree with me when I say this. But what does that mean? What is the meaning of a graced life? Grace is a topic that is much misunderstood by all too many Catholics. We were brought up on a view of grace that was woefully incomplete -- and incomplete in a way that had serious repercussions in our daily lives. Grace, we were told, was a quality or habit infused into the soul by God. It was a supernatural reality added to our nature. Grace was something we experienced at certain sacred moments. It was not something we experienced as a normal part of everyday life.

Contemporary theology has turned this whole understanding of grace around. It sees grace as the event of God's wondrous love offered to us at all times in our daily existence. Celebrating this Eucharist together opens us up to God gift of self. But when we leave this liturgy and go to the different responsibilities that call us, in each of them God's love is communicated to us. Paul in the reading from Romans speaks of God's love **poured** into our hearts. God's grace is ready to overwhelm us with its fullness. The only limit on that pouring out of God's love is our willingness to receive it. Thus Sr. Edwarda received that outpouring of God's grace, not simply when the Eucharist was brought to her. She received it in her moments of pain and suffering, as she waited God's final summons to come home. The grace of God's self-giving love was also present to those who watched and waited with her in her room. That room was a room aglow with God's wondrous gift of his love. Isn't this what Jesus is talking about in the Gospel when he offers us the invitation: "abide in my love." Jesus is the incarnate presence of God's love in our midst. He does not say that we would experience him on certain occasions. He wants us to abide in him, remain in his love, to live in that love.

I would not want to be misunderstood. What I say is not intended to deny the unique value of the sacramental moments in our lives and our need for them. What I do want to say is that we must not restrict the outpouring of grace, of God's love into our lives, to those moments alone.

I want this liturgy for this woman of graciousness and gratefulness to be a reminder to us that grace is a normal part of everyday life, not something added on. This special moment of liturgy – which we are now celebrating -- calls us to be open also to the constant presence of God's on-going self-giving that is such a wondrous ever-present reality in our lives – not just now, but at all times.

Can we perhaps take this ever- constant presence of God's love to us as one way of understanding the fullest meaning   contained in St. Edwarda's words to the bewildered thief: "God is my boss." Not an absentee one who is present only at times. The God she spoke of is a God who is everywhere with God's grace, God's self-giving love.

Sr. Gervase Kamas 10-14-2005

Readings: Is. 65:17-18
Philippians 1:19-21
Jn 14:1-7

I never got to know Sr. Gervase; I didn't know Sr. Protase either. I don't know anything about Saints Gervase and Protase. I looked them up and found that there is scant, if any, historical information about them. It is said that they were early martyrs, whose bones were discovered by St. Ambrose in Milan in 386. Ambrose's biographer says that they worked many miracles, including the restoration to sight of a blind butcher. Surely a very practical miracle for a butcher. Anyway, whatever can be said about their patron saints, we know that Sr. Gervase and Sr. Protase each had a history. We gather here to remember the story of Sr. Gervase.

I want to ask you now to take a moment to pretend, to imagine, something unusual occurring at this liturgy. Pretend that someone who knows nothing about Christian faith, but is curious about it, were to steal in here and break the silence that followed the reading of the Gospel by coming up here and asking: "What is it that you people are doing here?" Think for a moment what your answer would be to her question. Why *are* you here this afternoon? One answer we might give her could be this: we are here to celebrate in the ritual of the Mass an experience that we can never express fully in words. She might then ask: "What is this experience that you say you are here to celebrate that you can't express fully in words?" We could respond: "We are here to celebrate the death of Sr. Gervase." Our imaginary intruder by this time is quite perplexed: "What do you mean that you are here to *celebrate* her death? Was it that she was a problem that her removal will make life much easier for you? If not, then why don't you say that you're here to mourn her death?"

We would have to admit to her that, yes, there is something valid in what she says. When we say that we celebrate her death, this doesn't mean that there will be no grieving that a loved one has been taken from us. That would be uncaring, even unhealthy. Yes, there must be a sense of loss, but at the very heart of such a loss, there is the calming joy that faith brings: the calming joy of knowing that a life has achieved its fulfillment, that Gervase is now fully and forever in the embrace of divine love. Gervase has experienced resurrection. The life she now lives is risen life, so wonderfully different from the life she lived for so many years among her sisters.

It is death that makes all this possible for her – and for us. Hence we are here today not only to celebrate her death, but also to **look forward** to our own deaths. This statement would probably astound our bewildered intruder. She might want to say: "You don't actually mean that, do you? I know that death is inevitable and that we all have to face it at some time. But aren't you putting me on a bit when you say that you look *forward* to your deaths?"

In fact, at this point, you might all want to agree with her in thinking that I am pushing the envelope a bit when I suggest that we should **look forward** to our deaths.

Well, maybe. But listen to what Paul tells us: "For me to live is Christ and death is gain." What Paul is saying is that the only true life is life with God in Christ. Living with God in Christ is something that began for all of us the day we were baptized. That we can understand. That we can accept. Yes, with all our hearts we do want to live with Christ in God.

So we can identify with Paul when he says: "For me to live is Christ. But the second part of his statement – "death is gain" –that we find a bit more difficult to stomach. Faced with the prospect of death, we are a bit like St. Augustine, when he wanted to be a Christian, yet was not quite ready to give up the ways of the past. He prayed: "God make me chaste, but not yet." So we can say: "Yes, I want to appreciate that death is gain, but not yet. Fine for Gervase, but not for me – at least not yet."

I want to say quickly, before you tune me out, that I am not suggesting that – since Paul says "life is gain" – we should pray for an immediate death. I would point out, though, that those of us who say the Church's night prayer, say every night: "Grant us a restful night and a peaceful death." However, it is clearly not our intent that both come at once or at the same time.

What I want to suggest is that when we hear those words of Paul, they might lead us to change our perception of death. Death so often is seen simply as an evil, a physical evil. Yet this needs rethinking. It is dying, the process that leads to death, that is evil. It is sometimes painful, undignified, even terrifying. Different for each of us: for some almost painless, excruciatingly difficult for others. But whatever the process may be for us, it leads to death and death is gain.

Death is gain, not only because it takes us out of the process of dying. But because it is the supreme moment of human freedom. It ushers us into the immortal, glorious, everlasting phase of our existence. It brings new consciousness, new and abundant life.

This immortal life is mystery. It is hidden from us. And probably it is important that for now it remain hidden. For if we had an adequate understanding of what immortal life after death really is, that knowledge would trivialize life in the here and now. And that would be wrong. For this life is important: it is God's initial gift to us. And there are deeds God wishes us to accomplish. But God's ultimate gift of new life after death is the greatest gift of all, for it immerses us in God who is a boundless ocean of Mercy and Goodness and Love.

I must leave the last word to Sr. Gervase. She might want to say to our intruding guest: "I have to say: Bill doesn't really know what he is talking about. Oh, what he has said is true enough all right. But it falls so far short of the reality I am experiencing that it could just as easily be labeled untrue. I'd like to tell you about it, but human language just isn't capable of handling it. It would be like describing an electric light bulb to try to tell someone what the sun is. Just know that the experience surpasses all you have ever hoped for or dreamed about. And don't think that I have left you. I say this because I am not really in some place different from where you are. I am in God. But so are you. Thus, we are still together – in God. You don't realize that as fully as I do now. But it is so wonderfully true. And some day you will have that full realization too.'

And now what about our questioning intruder? Will she leave here with a better understanding of what we do when we gather here for a funeral liturgy? That's a question that each one of us has to answer. For there was no intruder. She is us. There is a bit of her and of her inquisitiveness in each one of us. It's an inquisitiveness that will be completely satisfied only when we join Gervase and Protase in the heavenly home Jesus has prepared for us.

Sr. Sarah Grundman 1-16-2006

Readings: Wis. 7:22-30
2 Cor. 4:16-18
Mt. 11: 25-30

Everybody loved Sarah. Everybody knew Sarah. Many, many people – more than we shall probably ever know – have been touched by Sarah – in her simple, quiet, loving way. Whatever your need, Sarah was always there for you. There was a sheer transparency about her. With Sarah, what you saw is what you got. She was a person you couldn't help but love. I smiled last night at the wake, when Sr. Florian's poem about Sarah was read. Sarah was not one to get too dressed up. Sr. Florian used to get furious with her for going into the sanctuary with her shirttails hanging out; yet her poem about Sarah showed how she too had fallen under the spell cast by Sarah's gentle goodness. And maybe it was not until we missed her physical presence among us that we could realize that somehow -- in a way we cannot explain -- she was larger than life. She was a Motherhouse institution. We are lessened because she has gone to God.

When I heard Thursday noon that Sarah had died, one of the first thoughts that entered to my mind was the title of a poem by Thomas Merton: "With the World in My Bloodstream." I thought of the many times for so many years that she needed to go to get blood transfusions. I wondered how many people unknown to her, people diverse in age and character, gave the blood that eventually flowed through her veins. She took so much blood in from others that she might well say: I live "with the world in my bloodstream." Yet all that blood -- from many different donors -- became one flow of life's blood in Sarah.

I want to use this fact that her body was able to integrate blood from many different sources into a unified whole as a symbol of Sarah's life. To quote from our first reading, there was about her a wisdom that "penetrated and pervaded all things." This suggests a simplicity about her life that refused to divide that life into various separate areas, isolated one from another. Her life was made up of so many diverse tasks, responsibilities, activities. She had care of the sacristy and the laundry. She was ground-keeper and gardener, horseback rider delighting in running to the fox hunt. She was golfer and bowler. She was handy person with tools who could fix most anything. Yet I would venture to say that, despite the many diverse activities she was involved in, her life was not a divided life. She moved easily from one area, one activity, to another. What made this possible was *her wonderful optimism that saw all of*

life as a single whole because all was a gift of God. There was no incongruity, therefore, in our spending a bit of time in the sacristy after Mass discussing her bowling scores, rejoicing when they were near 200 and lamenting when they were low. To be sure, she had her values straight. Clearly, getting a good score in bowling was not equal in importance to ministering to the altar for Mass; still, this did not mean that the bowling was unimportant. It was not to be trivialized, for it was all a part of one whole life.

If there is a lesson for us in Sarah's story -- and I think there is – it's a lesson of integration, of seeing life as a single whole that one must be grateful for -- as gift in its every aspect. All of us face the temptation of letting our lives get chopped up into different compartments, none of them connected with the others. It's as if we become a number of different persons at different times. If one could take a photo of our lives, they might resemble a bit a modern office in which each person, working in the same space, has her own cubicle marked off, and physically isolated from all the others.

There is a particular danger for people deeply committed to a life of spirituality: the danger of setting up a separate area of my life, labeled "my spiritual life." and then proclaiming it as the only one that really matters and hence must be kept separate from the rest of life.

What I think we can learn from the way Sarah moved so easily from one aspect of her life to another is the need we all have of recovering our basic natural unity and reintegrating our so often divided lives into a coordinated and unified whole, so that we become whole persons.

Sarah was a happy person. Life was for the living and she found joy in life. Joy in ridding the grounds of the pesky crows in the way only she knew how to do it; joy in a weekly clandestine hot dog roast with Carmelita down by the barn; joy in riding the horses and chasing the fox; joy in helping others – especially helpless people like me. I remember one time buying a bookcase that had to be assembled. When Sarah saw that my clumsy attempts resembled something Dagwood might have put together, she took pity on me and assembled it properly for me. It is still in my room today.

Sarah, you may know, personally chose all the readings for this liturgy. It's not difficult to understand why she chose the second reading: from Paul's second letter to the Corinthians. There is autobiography in her choice. Listen to it and think of Sarah: "We do not lose heart. Even as our body is being wasting away, our inner being is being renewed day by day." What an apt description of her. Sarah was no stranger to pain, as it invaded her person -- increasingly as time went by. Yet in the midst of it all she never lost sight of her deep, obedient, trusting faith that Jesus was at her side and that he meant it when he promised that his yoke is easy and his burden is light. For so long a time she had trouble with her blood level – taking courage when the blood level went up just a bit and enduring lightheartedly when it didn't.

Sarah, I offer this homily to you. Yet I have to say to everyone here that Sarah was her own best homily. For the essence of a homily is the proclamation of the good news. Sarah's life was a proclamation of good news: *the good news* about the daily life of a disciple of Jesus. The *good news* about being happy with the life situation in which God and circumstances have placed us, and accepting all that life brings -- embracing it generously and hopefully. The *good news* about offering a helping hand to our sisters and brothers. The *good news* of accepting the totality of life and all its elements as gifts from God. The *good news* of the sacredness of the mundane.

Roxanne, the hospice nurses' aide who was so faithful to Sarah, said that the moment before she died, a serene smile came over Sarah's face. Did she see what her whole life was preparing her for? Did she maybe see a familiar sign that read "Sarah's Place"? Once moved from 4095 East Avenue to 150 French Road, did she see it now in its final resting place? "Sarah's Place" --- is now totally with God.

SR. MARY LEE BISHOP 5-23-2006

Readings: 1Cor. 15:12-14
1 Jn 3:1-3
Lk. 22:39-46

Our responsorial psalm, psalm 23, is for many people the loveliest and most beloved of all the psalms. It highlights God's loving and gentle care for us. God cares for our every need, feeding us, anointing us, leading us to a place where we can rest and be refreshed. It's a consoling psalm, assuring us that God will always be with us. Yet in the very midst of that assurance of God's concern for us, there is what can only be called a discordant note. We pray:

"Though I walk through the valley of darkness, I fear no evil, for you are with me." The valley of darkness -- these words necessarily raise the disturbing question. Why must I go through the valley of darkness? Earlier in the psalm it says: "He leads me in right paths." Why must the right paths go *through* the valley of darkness? Why can't they go *around* the valley of darkness?

Confronting these questions puts us face to face with the mystery of evil, the mystery of incomprehensible suffering. And it must be said that the last years of Sr. Mary Lee's life force us to face these questions, not in some abstract, theoretical way, but in the lived experience of a gracious and loving woman whose life was full of accomplishments and talents that she so generously shared with others. We have to confront incomprehensible suffering in the life story of a wonderful Sister of St. Joseph, as that story unfolded and as the many extraordinary gifts she had been given – gifts she had so generously used to enrich the lives of many people – were, one by one, taken away. Until at the end even her power of vision was taken from her. She was no longer able to see. The darkness that enshrouded her was total. She was practically blind.

Those who knew Mary Lee before the darkness began to envelop her knew a loving, witty, gentle woman with a heart big enough to embrace all who entered into her world. I remember "the little girl from Groton," when she was a student at Nazareth College. Some students a teacher remembers because they were trouble-makers who gave you heart-burn. But there were also those whose eager responsiveness brought joy and warmth to your heart. A popular leader in her class and in the student body, Mary Lee was the kind of student a teacher dreams of having. In her senior year, she was chosen as May queen. She was also elected as prefect of the Sodality -- a distinguished honor in the days when the Sodality played an important role in the lives of Nazareth students. She was an excellent musician and an A-student who regularly appeared on the Dean's list of top students. When she first came here to 150 French Road to live with us, she would often say to me: "When I was in your class, I took down every word you said." I must admit that I shuddered a bit when she said that. She graduated in 1956. I am not sure I would want to subscribe today to what I might have said then. My one solace is the hope that those notes had long ago disappeared.

I return to the question her story demands that we face. Why was it necessary that this loving, gracious, talented woman should have to enter so deeply into the valley of darkness? We can face the fact that some bit of darkness enters into the lives of all of us. Our own experience confirms this. But why the extreme of suffering that was her lot? Why did she have to go so deeply into the valley of darkness that it seemed to envelop her whole being?

I have no answer to that disturbing question. But I do suggest an approach to it that in the long run will be more helpful than an answer. You will find it in today's Gospel reading. The Gospel is an account of Jesus' journey through the valley of darkness. The agony in the garden is a narrative that may serve as *the* paradigm for all Jesus' followers when they are called upon to deal with suffering that seems unbearable and so very unfair. Jesus anguishes over the bitter cup that he sees prepared for him. He shrinks from it. He prays that it be taken from him. The Letter to the Hebrews expresses it this way: "Jesus offered up prayers and supplications with loud cries and tears to the one who was able to save him from death." The text from Hebrews goes on to say "and he was heard because of his reverent submission."

Well, was his prayer heard? He prayed to be saved from death. Yet, as we know, he did die. Hence if you take his prayer and the response to it in literal terms, his prayer wasn't answered. He did die. But if you take the prayer and response in broader terms, his prayer was answered in a way that no one could have dreamed of. God did for Jesus something that had never before been experienced by a human being. God saved him from that which makes death a human necessity, namely mortality. Being delivered from mortality means that he was not simply brought back from the dead; he was brought into a life beyond death, a whole new kind of life: risen life. And risen life is something death can never touch. It is a life of joy and peace, a life of happiness and rest.

Jesus' death into life -- into new and immortal life -- is a paradigm pointing to some kind of meaning for what Mary Lee has had to experience during these years of suffering in body and in spirit. Does Jesus' story help us to deal with Mary Lee's story? The mystery of her suffering will always be there. But the parallel with Jesus' suffering can serve, I think, as a helpful way of gazing into that mystery.

We gather here today as a community of faith. What I have said about Mary Lee's story and its intertwining with Jesus' story demands a huge act of faith on our part. Do we believe in the resurrection? Do we believe that with Jesus something happened that had never happened before in human history? That because of Jesus a new human experience became a possibility for all God's people?

This is the challenge that our first reading demands that we face. Paul puts it clearly and bluntly: "If there is no resurrection of the dead, then Christ has not been raised. If Christ has not been raised, then our proclaiming it has been in vain and your faith has been in vain."

If I did not believe in the resurrection – Jesus' Mary Lee's, yours and mine – I would right now take off these vestments and leave this chapel and never return. Believing in the resurrection is that important – to me -- and I hope to all of us. Because we believe, we have the happy joyfulness of knowing that Mary Lee suffers no more and indeed enjoys a happiness so great that we have no vocabulary with which to describe it.

We are all aware that Mary Lee's death and the days before it have been difficult days for many people, especially Susan and also Mary Lee's ever faithful cousin, Jay as well as the many friends of Mary Lee and of Susan.

R. S. Thomas wrote a poem several years ago soon after his wife's death. He tells how, though she has left him, she comes to him still, impalpably and invisibly.

> There is a tremor
> Of light, as of a bird crossing
> The sun's path, and I look
> Up in recognition
> Of a presence in absence.
> Not a word, not a sound,
> As she goes her way
> But a scent lingering
> Which is that of time immolating
> Itself in love's fire.

Sr. Ruth Agnes Kesselring 3-23-2006

Is. 55: 1-3,10-11
1 Jn, 3:1-2
Jn. 15: 1-7

It was a wonderfully moving experience last Saturday as the graced history of the Congregation was unveiled. Stories are very important in our lives. It is by telling stories that we human beings make sense of our lives with its sorrows and its joys, its fears and hopes. Stories enable us to see that life is not just a series of unconnected events that happen to come together. Stories help us to see that our lives have meaning. They are going somewhere, -- of that we are convinced -- though there are times when our lives seem to be moving over a chasm of unknowing.

Seldom do we see with any real clarity where the story is leading us -- until we get there. In the meantime we have glimpses of enlightenment as a sense of where God's providence is leading us opens up for us a future fraught with possibilities we had not envisioned before.

Perhaps that is part of the meaning of that mysterious term we are hearing about so much these days: "refounding." Is refounding perhaps the opening up of new horizons for an old journey? As our second reading points out: "We are God's children now." That we know. That we are sure of. "But what we shall be has yet to be revealed." What the congregation of the Sisters of St. Joseph is yet to be is in the process of unfolding in a future radiant with hope.

That graced history wall tells the story of a congregation. It is a large story that embraces the many individual stories lived out over the years, indeed 350 years, by Sisters of St. Joseph. Today we enfold into that great story the narrative that Sr. Ruth Agnes Kesselring wrote in her seventy fruitful years in the Congregation.

And what a grand story it is! Ruth was a woman born to lead. She exercised leadership in the congregation, in the diocese of Rochester and in the lives of so many sisters whom her strong personality touched in ways both gentle and firm. She was a forward-looking woman. At a time when religious life was undergoing seismic changes, Ruth Agnes was a strong power for sanity and true humanness. She was a no-nonsense person who yet always enjoyed a good time. She was undaunted in standing up for what she believed. As superior at Sacred Heart convent when Bishop Casey was pastor of the cathedral, she was one of the few people who could stand toe to toe with Bishop Casey and not be the one to blink first. There was nothing petty about the way she dealt with people. She respected their humanness and their integrity. As Sr. Jamesetta said: "She had much to give to the congregation and she gave all.

Ruth Agnes was a woman of great courage. The word "courage" comes from the Latin word *cor* which means "heart." If courage depended on a highly active heart, Ruth would scarcely be a good candidate as a model of courage, since most of her heart had retired from action years ago. Her courage was a quality of her spirit. Courage is the ability to see things as they are. It's a willingness to look squarely and clearly at danger.

Courage is not foolheadness that ignores danger. A courageous person is one who understands her vulnerability, yet she refuses to let her life be governed by fear. At the same time she is not afraid to acknowledge her fears.

Twenty-seven years ago tomorrow, Archbishop Oscar Romero went to his martyr-death. I recall a story about him. He was chatting with a friend. He asked his friend: "Are you afraid to die?" Unhesitatingly, the friend said that he was not afraid to die. Oscar Romero admitted to him: "I am. I am afraid to die." And yet, when the time came, he did not hesitate to enter into a situation of grave danger that sent him to his martyr's death.

I remember one time asking Ruth: "Are you afraid to die?" She hesitated a moment: "I don't think I am afraid to die," she said. At that time she was not ready to make a firm statement one way or the other. But when the time came, she made the decision that only she could make: the decision to turn off the life-support system that had ceased to give her any benefit and was only causing her great distress. She made this decision with complete freedom -- and then waited for Jesus to come and take her home and escort her into risen life.

In this going home, in this entering into risen life, Ruth's life at last took on the fullness of meaning. For that is what resurrection is: it is the triumph of meaning. It was the triumph of meaning for Ruth, as it was also for the thousands of sisters whom we remember on our graced history wall.

On St. Joseph's day, when our graced history was unveiled, I was reminded of an event of some years ago. I gave a talk at the Memorial Art Gallery as part of a series on world religions. I recall that during the several days of this event, four Buddhist monks were working at a table building in sand a beautiful mandala -- a series of geometric figures in gorgeous colors. It was about the size of a huge birthday cake. It was a work of art produced by capable artists and with loving care and attention to detail. All who saw it marveled at the beauty.

Then on the final day of the conference, they carefully took the mandala, this beautiful work of art, to the river and dumped it into the water. The purpose of this ceremony was to highlight the impermanence of all reality. The message, as I understood it, was that nothing is lasting. Nothing remains forever.

This surely is in stark contrast to Christian belief in resurrection. It is our faith that God's love will not let us perish. Pope Benedict XVI, long before he became pope, wrote: "Men and women can no longer totally perish because they are known and loved by God. All love wants eternity, and God's love not only wants it but effects it."

All the particularity, all the uniqueness, that was Ruth Agnes continues to exist with a radiant beauty that comes from her union with the risen Lord Jesus.

She was a deeply prayerful woman. All through her life she did her best to answer Jesus' call to "abide" in Him. And that abiding is not just for a time, not just for an earthly lifetime. It is an abiding that lasts for all eternity.

Yes, Ruth's story has become part of the fullness of that graced history. Her story has been enfolded into the larger story of the congregation. But that is not all. The great story of this congregation is itself in the process of become part of a greater and grander story: namely, God's story. God's story is the story of the "refounding" of the human race in Jesus, in the life, death and resurrection of Jesus. This is the mystery of which Paul speaks: the mystery of God's plan to bring all things together in Christ.

As we incorporate Ruth's story into our graced history, the symbols on our history wall express our firm faith that that divine plan is in process of being achieved, as the human story moves – sometimes slowly, but yet irresistibly -- forward to the fullness of Christ's victory, when all will be one in God.

The future is radiant with hope.